St. Marys Public Library
100 Herb Bauer Drive
St. Marys, GA 31558

"La parole humaine est comme
un chaudron fêlé où nous battons
des mélodies à faire danser les
ours, quand on voudrait attendrir les
étoiles."

Gustave Flaubert
Madame Bovary

Front cover: *A typical bear, full of character! 1950.*

Page 1: *Tenderness with a hint of irony – the animal and his double. Drawing by Ellan, 1910.*

Previous page: *Childhood scene, 1935.*

Front jacket photograph by François-Xavier Bouchart.
Flap photographs by Max Barboni.

Geneviève and Gérard Picot

BEARS

Harmony Books / New York

Georgia Law requires Library materials to
be returned or replacement costs paid.
Failure to comply is a misdemeanor
punishable by law. (O.C.G.A 20-5-53)

688.724
P

Copyright © 1987 by Sté Nlle des Éditions du Chêne
Translation © 1988 by George Weidenfeld & Nicholson

All rights reserved. No part of this book may be reproduced or transmitted in any form or by any means, electronic or mechanical, including photocopying, recording, or by any information storage and retrieval system, without permission in writing from the publisher.
Published in the United States in 1988 by Harmony Books, a division of Crown Publishers, Inc., 225 Park Avenue South, New York, New York 10003 and represented in Canada by the Canadian MANDA Group.
Published in Great Britain by George Weidenfeld & Nicholson, 91 Chapham High Street, London SW4 7TA.
Originally published in France as *L'ours dans tous ses États* by Éditions du Chêne, 79 BD Saint-Germain 75288 Paris.
HARMONY and colophon are trademarks of Crown Publishers, Inc.
Manufactured in Italy
Design by Mark Walter

Library of Congress Cataloging-in-Publication Data
Picot, Geneviève.
Bears/by Geneviève and Gérard Picot.
p. cm.
Summary: Examines the history of teddy bears, their relationship to their owners, and their niche in the world of art.
1. Teddy bears. [1. Teddy bears.] I. Picot, Gérard. II. Title.
NK8740.P54 1988
688.7'24—dc19
ISBN 0-517-57063-7
10 9 8 7 6 5 4 3 2 1
First Edition

414987

CONTENTS

THE BIRTH AND EARLY HISTORY OF THE KING OF STUFFED TOYS

The teddy bear, that cherished companion of both the young and old, seems always to have been around, played with by generations of children as far back as anyone can remember. Surprisingly, he is just eighty-five years old. Since his invention in 1903, this much-loved creature has seen countless children through the traumas of growing up and entertained so many others with his exploits in cartoons, films and story-books, that he has achieved an almost legendary status and deserves to be treated with a little dignity and respect. In folktales, legends and fairy stories from around the world, the bear has proved an enduring and popular hero. In more recent years the adventures of Winnie-the-Pooh, Paddington, and Rupert – translated into many languages – have become minor literary classics which deserve a place on every child's bookshelf. Prosper and Gros Nounours from France, and Michka, the hero of Russian folk tales, are but a few of the other famous bears whose antics have delighted both adults and children alike, and will no doubt continue to do so. Likewise, the teddy bear, that patched and tattered toy, has become an international star. Such is his appeal that he has become the subject of exhibitions and a much sought after commodity: the oldest and rarest specimens now fetch high prices at auction. His story is a mysterious and magical one.

Left: *U.S.A., 1905. The child's uniform seems to hint at Teddy Roosevelt.* Right: *With his snout in the air and his sparkling eyes, the teddy bear never sleeps; he is always on the alert.* Previous page: *A torrent of teddies in the 1980s.*

Exactly where the teddy bear first appeared seems to have confused more than one genealogist, as London, Württemberg and Brooklyn all lay claim to being his birthplace during 1903. The English cling to the idea that teddy bears were named after King Edward VII – himself nicknamed Ted – who was reputedly charmed by the bears at London Zoo. But generally speaking, those who place some store on proof feel that this story is too simplistic and lacks any element of substantiated fact. There are arctophiles (from the Greek *arctos*, meaning bear) who thoroughly enjoy endless discussions on the origin of the teddy bear and his name, whether or not they ever reach a satisfactory conclusion. However, by far the most popular version of how the teddy bear came into being maintains that his true father was T.R. . . . Theodore Roosevelt, former President of the United States of America.

So, let us go back some eighty-five years into the past to discover the truth behind this famous story. Theodore Roosevelt was a keen sportsman and well known for his love of hunting. On finding himself in the south to investigate a frontier dispute between Louisiana and Mississippi, he leapt at the chance of indulging in one of his favourite pastimes – bear hunting. In those days, ecology was seldom a matter for concern; bears, regarded as vicious predators, were legitimate targets for the hunter and could be shot indiscriminately without incurring the wrath of the S.P.B. (Society for the

DRAWING THE LINE IN MISSISSIPPI
1902

Protection of Bears). Roosevelt, who up until then had not even bagged the smallest bear skin, felt honour bound – given his position – to leave with a trophy; his hosts, who also had a sense of diplomacy, felt equally obliged to provide him with one. They accordingly came up with the idea of tying up a young bear with a rope and shouting out to Roosevelt: 'A bear, Mr President, a bear!' On emerging from his tent at this commotion, the president found himself nose to nose with the poor little bear cub who had all too clearly been prepared for sacrifice. Having no real taste for an easy victory, Roosevelt viewed his hosts' seriousness with profound contempt. However, sensing that here was a situation that, in the eyes of the media, he could shrewdly turn to his advantage he uttered his now famous remark: 'If I killed this little bear, I could never look my children in the eye again.'

Top: *Bear hunting, President Teddy Roosevelt's great passion.* Bottom right: *'If Theodore is the President of the United States with his clothes on, what is he in the nude? A Teddy bare!'* Bottom left: *The cartoon by Berryman which started the teddy bear craze.*

According to another version of the story, the president's victim was a great old fat bear, left prey to the hunter out of sheer exhaustion. Once again, pride and a sense of fair play meant that he could not countenance such a killing in the name of sport and so Roosevelt ordered that the poor animal should be put out of its misery. Witnessing this event was the political cartoonist Clyfford Berryman who sketched the scene and published the drawing shortly afterwards in the *Washington Star*. It was accompanied by the caption: 'Drawing the line in Mississippi'. This carried two connotations: one was political, referring to the thorny problem of the frontier between the two states, the other ideological, portraying Theodore Roosevelt, known as an enthusiastic supporter of black civil rights, refusing to shoot at the bear – a black one – which had been brought to him, tied at the neck. Perhaps influenced by the legendary goodwill that bears are often supposed to inspire in people, Clyfford Berryman waived all copyright, coming up with the memorable phrase: 'I have made thousands of children happy, and that's enough for me.' The drawing proved to be so popular that it made Berryman's reputation as a political cartoonist: appropriately enough, he was later to use the bear as his signature.

At this point in the story the teddy bear existed only on paper: it was to take the imagination and foresight of the owner of a small Brooklyn sweetshop to bring him to life. Morris Michtom, a Russian immigrant, was always on the lookout for new ideas and products which would tempt his customers and help his business to prosper. Realizing that diversification was the key to success, he had already thought of using the shop to display the toys and dolls that his wife made. However, it was Berryman's cartoon that was to give him the inspiration for the product that was to revolutionize the toy world and make Michtom both rich and famous. Perhaps fondly reminded of the bears in his native homeland, Michtom transformed the pathetic bear cub in the drawing into a brown plush toy that was given pride of place in the window next to Berryman's cartoon. In no time at all this first example was sold – the teddy bear was born.

From that moment on Mrs Michtom scarcely had a moment's rest: orders flooded in and bears were being sold almost before they had been made. Morris Michtom, a shrewd businessman, realized that he had to capitalize upon this success and had the bright idea of naming his new toy after the president. In a

Right: *A family of Art Deco bears, from a drawing by Maby, 1920.* Bottom: *A baby bear and a bear the size of a baby.* c. *1905.* Left: *A nostalgic boot-button gaze. How sweet it is to have a friend, as precious as he is small. United States,* c. *1910.*

state of great excitement and anticipation the Brooklyn shopkeeper designed and made up a bear specially for presentation to the White House, accompanying it with his request. The couple waited nervously to see what the outcome would be. The reply was quick and positive, though qualified: 'I don't believe that my name will do much for the image of your stuffed bear, but you have my permission to use it.' This false modesty – or lack of commercial foresight – from the president did not deter Michtom, who dreamed happily of a successful future for his invention. Putting his ideas into practice he soon found his order book filling up and the demand for the bear exceeding his wildest expectations. As sales grew, Michtom decided to sell his idea to the Ideal Toy Corporation – still one of America's largest toy manufacturers. At that time, there was no such thing as a patent and Morris was unable to protect his simple, yet brilliant idea. Tempted by his success, other manufacturers were quick to jump on the bandwagon and by 1910 dozens of companies were making bears of all shapes and sizes. When Michtom died in 1938 the White House sent a letter of condolence to his family, and many mourned the loss of the little Brooklyn shopkeeper who gave the world one of its most popular and endearing toys.

Top: *Richard Steiff, inventor of the first German bear.* Bottom: *Portrait of Margarete Steiff, with the symbol of her success on her knee.* Right: *The teddy bear at the start of his reign: boot-button stare, protruding snout and rigid pose.*

However, at the same time, on the other side of the Atlantic, the Germans were busy creating their own version of the teddy bear and adding to the mystery concerning his true origins. In this instance the teddy bear's creator was a young paralysed girl. Margarete Steiff lived in Giengen, an industrial town of tanners and weavers in a poor part of Germany. Despite her handicap, which confined her to a wheelchair, Margarete was determined to make a living for herself. Helped by a courageous character and luck (Giengen was the place where the sewing machine had been invented and also a centre of felt manufacture) she began to make children's clothes. One day a picture of an elephant caught her eye and so gave her the idea for a highly original pincushion – a stuffed animal in the shape of an elephant in which pins could be stuck. These elephants soon became playthings and inspired Margarete to make other stuffed animals.

Margarete was enthusiastically supported in her ventures by the whole of the Steiff family who all wanted to share in her success. Her brother was the first to take a large quantity of the toys to market where he sold every one, but back in the workshop help came from every

Top: *A production line in America as the teddy bear craze hits the States: the mohair bear is a big favourite.* Right: *One of the very first teddy bears.* Left: *Factory scene near Birmingham. British bear production began later than in both Germany and America. These handsome bears were produced during a twelve-hour working day.* Following page: *Bears became more rounded and squat in the 1940s.*

Right: *Young girl dressed as a fairground gypsy with her 'dancing bear'.* Left: *Photograph in the style of Lewis Carroll,* c. *1920.*

quarter. Her five nephews soon joined the ranks: one responsible for researching and developing new ideas, another looking after business matters, another tackling technical aspects, another – even at this early stage – handling publicity and promotion, and finally, the fifth, Richard Steiff, a poet who spent his time sketching the bears at Stuttgart zoo. It was Richard, a student at Giengen's technical college, who proposed to his aunt the idea of a toy bear with entirely new features. This one would no longer be made of felt, but instead would have long hair and a moveable head and limbs.

Exhibited in Leipzig in 1903, this latest addition to the Steiff family of toys

Left: *Advertisement from an American catalogue,* c. *1910.* Right: *American bear hug,* c. *1905.* Following page, left: *1940s bear, with exterior jointing in leather, embroidered snout and boot-button eyes.* Right: *A clown bear from 1940, who has lost none of his bounce; he has prominent embroidered eyes and a rather worn two-tone coat. Though his paws stick out, they are not jointed.*

failed to enjoy the success that had been anticipated. He seemed destined to be a failure until, at the last minute on the final day of the fair, an American stopped in front of the stand. Richard showed him his most popular products, but all to no avail, for the customer wanted to take home an entirely novel and different sort of toy. Suddenly, the previously neglected bear caught his eye, won him over, and resulted in him placing an immediate order for 3,000 similar bears. The order was met without delay and the fabric bear quickly became the Steiffs' trademark, despite the indifference of the European public. The final twist in the tale comes, however, when this same American buyer exhibited the bears in New York where, quite by chance, they were spotted by the designer responsible for the prestigious task of decorating the tables at Theodore Roosevelt's daughter's wedding reception. Not wanting to miss any opportunity of displaying some witty originality amongst his decorations, he immediately invested in one of the little brown bears. Remembering the president's love of hunting – bear hunting in particular – the guests at the wedding joked about the 'Teddy' bear. Thus the teddy bear was born, the teddy bear boom was launched and the two stories surrounding his creation appear to become one. However, when the late Peter Bull, a renowned English collector, asked Alice Roosevelt about the details surrounding this last part of the legend, he found

Looking at the earliest stuffed bear, we may indeed wonder why he became such a success, spawning such a flourishing family and enjoying such remarkable longevity.

On first encountering him, one may be surprised by his sad and fatalistic demeanour. His green eyes are bulging and almost frightening, but they still tug at the heart strings. Surely it must have been this fascinating stare which made him one of childhood's best-loved characters, for the rest of his body has little appeal.

He is a dumpy creature, small and stiff, with short mousey-grey fur; he has a crabby expression and he is densely stuffed with wood shavings, giving him a rather upright, military bearing. With his

Top right: *Reproduction of the first Steiff bear, manufactured in 1983 to celebrate the company's eightieth anniversary.* Left: *Teddy bear with cotton coat, exterior jointing, long snout and boot-button eyes, dating from the 1940s.*

pleasant to touch. We feel like manipulating him or playing with him rather than stroking him. He just does not seem to encourage tenderness and yet. . . . Children must have felt a really overwhelming need for some sort of contact

narrow shoulders, his broad waist, his long arms firmly by his side and his snout in the air, he holds himself perfectly for inspection: he seems more fit to join a troop of tin soldiers in a military march-past than to spend his nights cradled in a child's arms. His body's few curves are limited to his tiny ears and a venerable hump which confirms his pedigree. His embroidered mouth, in its rather tart outline, like an inverted 'v', gives him a diffident and haughty pout. He is a model of self-discipline; only when turned upside down is his impeccable poise disrupted as a despairing mooing sound issues forth.

As for his texture, he is made out of tufted mohair which, though of outstanding quality, is so short and stiff that he is actually rather unpleasant to touch.

for them to have adopted him so readily in so spartan a form.

With greater pragmatism, adult enthusiasts have transformed him into a speculative collectors' item: these venerable grandfathers of today's teddy bears have already appeared at auction. Indeed, even worse, the 6,000 reproductions of the first teddy bear, manufactured in 1983, were sold out in only a few weeks. The man who created this little creature can surely never have imagined that such an illustrious future lay ahead of his protégé.

out that she hated stuffed bears – a fact which she demonstrated by showing him photographs of the wedding with not a bear in sight. Whether he is American or German however, whether he was present at Alice Roosevelt's wedding reception or not, the stuffed bear was born, and is still alive and well, now celebrating his eighty-fifth birthday.

The fascinating story of the birth of the teddy bear seems to contain elements of both the ultimate rags-to-riches success story and the perfect fairy-tale – the American self-made man and the tragic yet triumphant heroine. Morris Michtom's story is one of a Russian immigrant for whom the United States offered boundless opportunities. His ambition to succeed transformed him from a small-time confectioner into a rich and famous man. He recognized a good opportunity, had a nose for fashion, a love of risk, an alert head for business and a sense of timing which allowed him to transform a caricature glimpsed in a newspaper into an enormously popular product. His opportunism took him to the White House and his success was assured. In contrast to this commercialism, the story of Margarete Steiff is a fairy-tale within a fairy-tale. A paralysed young girl succeeded through talent and ingenuity in overcoming the limitations of her handicap and rose from her humble beginnings in a poor industrial town to become the inspiration behind a thriving business catering to worldwide demand. In 1983, when the very first Steiff bear was re-issued, he once again became the focus of enthusiastic attention. The public always have and probably always will enjoy a story with a happy ending, which explains the popularity of these stories and will ensure, whether they are true or not, that they continue to be told.

Top left: *German teddy bear, 1950, with long mohair coat and glass eyes.* Right: *Bear made of velvet, France, 1920. During the Jazz Age, bears responded to the prevailing mood and went multi-coloured.* Bottom left: *Later, though still jointed, bears became more rounded; this French one, for example, dates from 1930.* Right: *France, 1950: one of the last bears still to have an embroidered nose, before the advent of plastic.*

A Brief Outline of the Evolution of the Teddy Bear

During the first ten years of his existence, the earliest teddy bear's lanky and rather inflexible shape made him easy to recognize. When standing, he seemed stiff and imperious, his boot-button gaze staring his owner in the eye with an uncompromising call to attention; when seated, he was all arms, ready to grab hold of someone in an embrace. If he had been the wolf encountered by Little Red Riding Hood, she would doubtless have asked him: 'But why are your arms so long?', to which he would have certainly replied: 'All the better to hug you with, my child!' In profile, he was very much of a stereotype, his most prominent feature a protruding muzzle which dominated the space around him. However, because there was still concern at this stage about realistic detail, there was a hump at the top of his back which offset this. The mobility and independence of his limbs compensated for a certain physical impoverishment and allowed his pivoting head to turn and stare at his hump, while his paws and arms could move about at will. Exterior jointing was left naïvely visible, and the clasps at the shoulders and waist produced unavoidable dents. A more sophisticated system of interior jointing was provided by balls of stiff cardboard attached to a frame. The earliest models often sported a mohair coat, though this surface display of affluence concealed the comparative poverty of their stuffing, generally composed of wood fibres, sawdust or kapok.

The immediate runaway success of these first bears led many doll manufacturers to fear that *their* sales would plummet in the face of growing demand for this popular new toy. In America one firm even launched a publicity campaign whose message was nothing if not explicit: 'A stuffed bear is a toy but a doll is a doll, which every little girl wants and needs.'

The bear family grew rapidly in size as new versions were manufactured in a variety of sizes and shades of brown, mainly originating in Germany and the United States. They acquired their characteristic glass eyes around 1910 but, in the years following the First World War, realism lost some ground as the bear's mohair coat, previously produced in a range of tones from light honey to dark brown, was increasingly manufactured in unnatural colours. Some bears, made out of velvet or thick flannel, even brazenly sported red coats in shades varying from vermillion to ruby. Competition soon led to distinctive new styles being developed. Although the teddy bear retained his slim outline, from around 1920 clown-style bears appeared, in contrasting or asymmetrically arranged colours. The Twenties marked an important turning-point in the history of the stuffed bear for it is only then that they made their first appearance in France. Before the Great War, France had imported teddy bears mainly from Germany, but afterwards, when supplies dried up, there was a gap in the market which encouraged the French to create their own version. The Thiennot company had an outstanding year in 1919: not only was the business established during that year, but they also produced the first French stuffed bear, which won a bronze medal in competition.

A huntsman's outfit helps to finish off a docile and much-loved grizzly, c. 1910. The teddy bear shares his owner's wildest, childhood adventures and fate's hardest knocks; whether active or passive, he is by turn actor and accomplice.

During the 1930s, the teddy bear's limbs grew shorter as he took on a rounded outline and became more squat (though he still had a hump on his back). This development is generally regarded to be due to the popularity of the celebrated English bear, Winnie-the-Pooh, whose tubby figure greatly influenced manufacturers. More often than not the teddy bear was jointed, but around this time a new all-in-one version emerged who would soon challenge the original bear in the popularity stakes: with chubby arms and hips, his head sitting firmly on top of his shoulders, his shape had become well and truly rotund. In 1937 the French company ALFA (*Articles de Luxe et de Fabrication Artisanale*) designed a bear whose upper part alone could be moved while his short legs and protruding feet stood firmly on the ground. At the same time, the bear's features became once more a subject for concern as, for instance, a clearer distinction emerged between the sexes.

During the war years between 1939 and 1945, lack of raw materials led to a greater reliance on the imagination and on those few resources that were available. At home women cut, sewed and put together *anything* that could feasibly be used to make soft toys. Manufacturers, similarly restricted, did not give in completely, however, and the bears produced during this lean period had to be adapted according to circumstances. Strangely enough, at this time there were no quotas for the importation of Algerian sheepskins and so, by an ironic twist of fate, the bears made from this material assumed the guise of an

404/5

Steiff
IM OHR

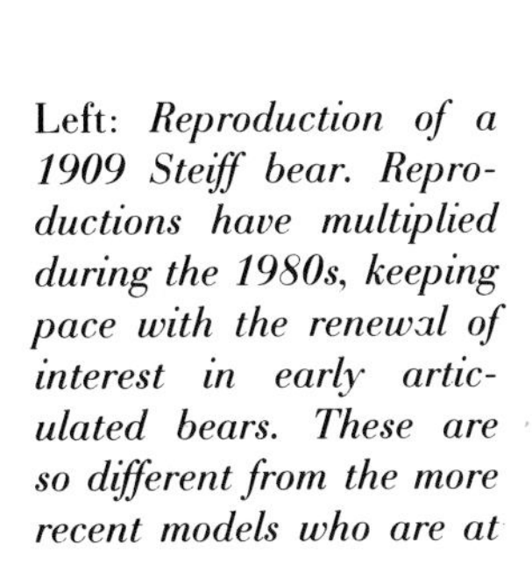

Left: *Reproduction of a 1909 Steiff bear. Reproductions have multiplied during the 1980s, keeping pace with the renewal of interest in early articulated bears. These are so different from the more recent models who are at best soft and furry and at worst limp and spineless.* Above: *British bears, 1940 and 1980. During the 1970s and 1980s bears have become softer and more rounded, losing their earlier degree of realism.* Left: *French bear, 1940.*

animal they might more naturally be inclined to attack. The ones that did not have this long woollen coat generally felt rather cold and smooth, like oilskin.

During the 1950s, while some bears became softer both in their shape and in the material from which they were made, others rather took a turn for the worse and became less attractive. The bear lost his hump and his snout gradually shortened so that eventually it became squat enough to give him a

Left: *Shirley Temple in the arms of a bear whose size matches that of her reputation. Her fans throughout the world sent teddy bears to her.* Right: *Anonymous starlet of the Fifties with a more modestly sized companion, whom she none the less hugs enthusiastically.*

bulldog-like expression. Nose in the air, bad-tempered, truculent, looking for a fight – there was nothing particularly attractive in his scowling appearance for he looked just like a boxer transformed into a miniature plaything.

Jointed bears, still in the majority, existed alongside new, larger types; slowly materials changed and artificial fur was introduced. Glass eyes and embroidery – which gave relief to his face – were gradually replaced by moulded plastic eyes and noses, which was a significant development in the evolution of the species. In 1954, the Boulgom company launched a revolutionary bear in which latex was used for the stuffing, making him softer and more supple. This bear was still jointed, but was rendered more pliable as his previously rigid insides (made of bran or straw) were replaced by this new rubber material. With his new warmth and softness this amenable toy was a far more suitable recipient of a child's affectionate confidences.

The introduction of latex stuffing in the 1950s made a considerable difference to the bear's softness and weight. Here are a jointed bear and one moulded in one piece. France, Boulgom, 1953. Inset: *As a guardian angel, the teddy bear helps the child to overcome his fear of the dark and to sleep at night.*

During the 1960s the public became concerned about health and safety standards for toys; synthetic fur tended to be inflammable, noses and eyes offered little resistance to inquisitive fingers, and the dyes used in toys could stain children's tongues. Something clearly had to be done about this and so standards were set for chemicals, strength and durability of materials, as well as for non-flammability, so as to prevent a child's plaything from turning into his killer.

During the '70s and '80s, the teddy bear became chubbier, softer and lighter. He also became more elaborate and more colourful. Unlike the way that man evolved from the ape, the bear, as stuffed toy, has taken rather a different path: he has developed from an upright-standing animal into a dumpy, rounded one. But, like man, his technological mastery has increased: the cleverest toys can now speak, recognize a familiar voice, change colour in hot water, or even react to body heat (the unbridled imagination of certain manufacturers in trying to create sensational new inventions has occasionally unleashed some degenerate creations into society!). Flabby and spineless and dressed in 'Hollywood' colours, these bears are unworthy descendants of their honourable ancestors. But despite changing fashions, some people insist that they are still bears, and that even though they are soft and malleable, they still remain true to their origins. Despite the popularity of these latest bears, the manufacture of jointed versions has continued, and of late there has been a resurgence of interest from collectors for this type of bear. Always with bright black eyes – or eyes with a pupil and coloured iris – the teddy bear has never been fitted with a doll's moving eyelid mechanism and thus never sleeps. Whether made of boot buttons, trouser buttons, glass, painted porcelain or plastic, you cannot avoid a teddy bear's piercing stare as he doggedly surveys life around him, people and things. Almost seeming to scorn the darkness and gloom when day turns into night, he stares obstinately ahead and watches out for intruders.

Any historical account can be a little vague in parts. It is particularly difficult to date and name teddy bears, for many reasons; the loss of archives, bankruptcy, plagiarism or simply a lack of interest from owners in recording these details all contribute to that aura of mystery that surrounds certain aspects of the teddy bear's evolution.

H Schmidt.

PAST LEGENDS AND PRESENT-DAY MYTHS

What a curious fate the bear has had! Brown or white, this wild and ferocious predator ranging over parts of the countryside as undisputed master, terrorizing man and beast, finds himself transformed into a cuddly toy sitting on the shelves of every little town toyshop or dangling disconsolately by the cash till of the smallest service station.

The bear in the wild is a little like a Jekyll and Hyde character: lumbering and rather docile in appearance he will still probably attack when provoked. An innocent Canadian woman, not content simply to stand and admire a bear she encountered during a walk in the country, was attacked and she lost an arm. After this accident, the young lady felt moved to speak out in the press against the 'bruin myth', which misleads people into believing that the bear is a good-natured animal when he is, in fact, a wild and dangerous one. This savage, untameable beast would scarcely recognize his harmless domesticated double. The teddy bear is the star of stuffed toys. Number one in the top fifty bestsellers, he does not give rise to the sexist feelings which other toys often provoke – everybody loves him. To demonstrate this point a study was carried out in France involving five hundred children. They were shown a menagerie of stuffed animals, both wild and domesticated. Fifty per cent stopped in front of the bear and pointed him out. How and why has a beast like the bear become such a popular toy? What has he done to deserve such attention and admiration? It has to be said that there is quite a discrepancy between the animal itself and its soft, cuddly counterpart, which quietly shares a bed with so many children (and no small number of grown-ups!).

Left: *Samivel's 'Brun l'Ours'.* Right: *Seymour Eaton's Roosevelt Bears, created in 1905 as a result of the phenomenon known as the 'Teddy Bear craze'.* Previous page: *In legends the bear has a reputation for being a great lover, much appreciated by women.*

Man and Bear

In naming bears – real or imaginary – man even goes so far as to give him human Christian names such as 'Rupert' or 'Teddy'. Moreover, just as man gives the bear the names of his own kind, so man himself can be described as 'bear-like' if his fellows find him surly. Similarly, a man can be said to be 'like a bear with a sore head' if he is openly rude or disagreeable. Gustave Flaubert, the nineteenth-century French novelist, was described as 'rather a character, a bit of a bear, by no means an ordinary man'.

Though man evolved from the apes, he could almost have done so from the bear (may Darwin forgive us!), for the bear can claim – far more legitimately – to have broken through the barrier which separates mankind from the animal world. In shape and appearance, the bear is

The Man with the Dancing Bear

He was standing beneath the canopy of stars, his eyes wide, his open mouth gaping at the sky as if he were trying to drink the Milky Way. Slowly, he swayed his shoulders to and fro. A heavy moan rose from his cavernous chest, continuing on two notes for hours on end. Gaston listened, lying on his back with his hands behind his head, his gaze lost in the vastness of the skies. Towards the north, he could make out the oblong shape of Ursa Minor and Ursa Major, the mother bear.

'Can you see the bear, Marti?' Gaston said, for his companion's benefit. 'Can you see your mother in the sky?'

His nose straining towards the sky, the bear was still intoxicated by the stars. His song was as profound as could be imagined; the link was made. The bears were swimming in the female forces of the universe. The mother bear filled the heavens while Marti's deep-throated moan welled up from the bowels of the earth. [. . .]

Leading a bear amongst men was a truly sacred calling; it was the marriage of Heaven and Earth.

Gaston was a bear man, a showman of bears. [. . .] Bringing men into contact with bears, he was 'one of the earth's high priests'. He knew it now, but he would not let it go to his head. He was still ordinary and straightforward. He was still a peasant from the mountains, Gaston Sentien from Ercé. Like a true warrior who knows that he is only a medium for powers coming from elsewhere, he was careful to avoid feelings of pride or greed. He knew full well that if he succumbed to either his heart would become hard and the miracle would be snuffed out.

Jean Fléchet, *Le Montreur d'ours.*

Top: *Pyreneen huntsmen in 1950: bear hunting was finally banned in 1957.* Bottom: *Bear showmen, c. 1910. The popularity of their performance was enhanced by the bear's reputation as a sacred and magical beast.* Right: *Illustration by J.-M. Nicollet for Editions Gallimard: the bear hunt as a struggle against a mythical beast.*

undeniably close to man. His posture, gestures and character fascinate us because they display characteristics similar to our own.

Not only do bears resemble us in appearance, they do so in their way of life too, and in this respect there is one biological activity similar to man's that needs to be mentioned: sex. The earliest observations of this activity in bears can be traced back as far as Pliny, who noted that bears copulate '*more ferrarum*', in other words facing each other, rather than in the more common animal fashion. Gaston Phoebus's zoological commentaries in the *Livre de la chasse* also note this anomaly: 'When the male bear performs his task with a female bear, they behave like a man and woman, lying one on the other.' Like man, the bear too appears to take enjoyment in this activity, but more frequently he likes to abandon himself to a no less important pleasure . . . his love of food. In addition to the fact that like man, the bear is omnivorous, he is also one of the few animals openly to display his enjoyment of eating. Many children's stories celebrate this touching weakness that the bear has for food and for the taste of honey in particular – Michka, desperate to open the pot of honey he finds in the forest; Winnie-the-Pooh who, on the stroke of eleven, could always eat 'a little something'; the 'Roosevelt Bears' who astonished their audience with their incredible capacity for food; and Paddington, who would sell his soul for a pot of marmalade.

With an appetite for both honey and girls, men and bears are both rivals for the same territory. Inset: *If oral tradition and folk tales are to be believed, bears ravish women in order to live with them as husband and wife: this Pyreneen carnival acts out the scene.*

All too often the bear is portrayed as clumsy and naïve, suggesting that man has perhaps used literature as a form of revenge against an animal who in reality can act with much greater subtlety. In fact, to satisfy his craving for food, the bear is capable of employing considerable cunning and trickery. An extremely wary and shrewd animal, the bear never returns to the scene of previous slaughters and has been known to follow extraordinarily circuitous paths in pursuit of things he craves, a talent which also enables him to throw huntsmen off his trail. In the words of a Turkish proverb: 'For every huntsman's trick, the bear has an escape route.'

Hibernation is the bear's most distinctive biological trait: when autumn comes around, he digs himself a hole about fifty centimetres deep which he lines with vegetation for warmth and comfort. Turning his back on the world, the bear settles himself in and waits for spring. This behaviour has always fascinated man who, feeling an affinity with the bear, perhaps wishes he could do likewise. Gustave Flaubert, for instance, at his lair at Croisset, had a bearskin rug gracing his study floor and also wished to buy 'a handsome bear (in oils) to hang framed in the bedroom with the caption: Portrait of Gustave Flaubert showing my moral outlook and social attitudes.' His contempt for the stupidity of the contemporary world made him 'become more bearlike every day'. Yet it is not only hibernation which prompts man to identify with the bear, it is also the animal's thick, furry coat which protects him from the outside world. At a particularly difficult time in his life, Flaubert congratulated himself on his 'three-layered pelt'. The theme recurs in the novel *The Hotel New Hampshire* where John Irving describes a woman who dresses in a bear costume, and whose behaviour is, at the very least, ambiguous. The psychological interest in the character hinges on the changing and equivocal game she

NOUGAT DE L'OURS GOURMAND
Ets PONCET, PIALLAT, TEYSSEIRE
CRÉATION R. MARTIN LYON
L'OURS GOURMAND
VÉRITABLE NOUGAT DE MONTÉLIMAR
ÉTABLISSEMENTS PONCET, PIALLAT, TEYSSEIRE

plays as Susie the bear and Susie the woman, although the fact that she can only confront the world by donning a bearskin points to some more basic psychological difficulties.

Not only do man and bear resemble each other in some respects (or almost), but they also have a mutual love-hate relationship. Man, for his part, has always hunted and killed bears, from prehistoric times right up to the present-day grizzly bear hunts which so excite latter-day Davy Crocketts, who make up in weaponry for what they lack in courage. For those willing to pay the price, helicopters will herd the animals within range of a rifle equipped with telescopic sights.

The late Marshall Tito, for example, was a great aficionado of bear hunting and had a swing chair mounted in an observation platform so that he could shoot at bears with an ultra-sophisticated carbine while comfortably reclining on a cushion. . . . He does not hold the record for this sport, however, as in 1978 alone, Ceaucescu managed to kill no fewer than 213 bears. It is not only heads of state who have indulged in this sport, though, as Alaska and some Eastern bloc countries still extend a warm welcome to fanatical huntsmen in search of a trophy to drape over their beds. In contrast, the bear is not spontaneously aggressive towards man and only attacks when seriously provoked. Yet man has happily perpetuated the notion that the reverse is true, concocting endless stories about bears' violent behaviour. In a popular Russian tale, *The Bear who lost a Paw*, an old lady meets a particularly horrifying end after taking advantage of a sleeping bear to provide herself with some meat for a stew: upon waking, the now amputated bear tracks the woman to her home, decapitates her and eats her.

Right: *Flaubert, who once said of himself: 'I am a bear and, like a bear, want to stay in my lair, in my cave, in my skin, in my old bearskin, quiet and free from the ladies and gentlemen of the bourgeoisie.'* Bottom corner: *Prosper, Saint-Ogan's hero, who would have approved of Flaubert's sentiments.*

But we should not look only on the black side for the bear shares other, less violent, human characteristics. According to a number of sources, ranging from the visual imagery and literature of the medieval period, to present-day newspaper reports in Turkey, the Andes and Siberia, the bear has always proved attractive to women. It seems that he has been accused less of eating lambs and indiscriminately pillaging beehives than of making off with shepherdesses and young girls. The myth of the bond between women and bears has been used to salacious effect in the European oral tradition, and the medieval imagination created a rich and varied mythology around sexual commerce between men and bears. In numerous stories, bears are said to carry off young girls whom they then imprison in their lairs and treat as their own wives. Their union produces unusual yet charming offspring, whose whole life revolves around being different. They appear to be half-man, half-animal, but enjoy almost god-like powers (as in the *Conte de Jean l'Ours*, for example, where the hero is presented as a serious rival to his human brother). But the bear does not simply make off with women for his own pleasure, tearing them away from any enjoyment of life. At the beginning of his cohabitation, the bear is careful not to treat his new partner roughly, as if she were merely a prisoner. According to the legends, he tries to win her over by doing all he can to make her happy and satisfy her every need. 'Although he was a bear, he was a real

husband' – are the words repeated over and over again by the young woman, when freed from the captivity of her clumsy but sensitive lover.

Honey and Pancakes too

It is interesting to consider the way in which the bear seems to function according to the same seasonal clock as man. Surely there is nothing to suggest that our readings of the sun and moon's movements are anything more than coincidentally linked with the bear's chosen days for doing things? The hibernation season invariably begins on the Feastday of St Martin, but the bear's behaviour on Shrove Tuesday is even more interesting, for it is supposed to enable us to predict the rest of the winter's weather. During early February the bear wakes up and gets ready to leave his cave for the first time in months. Snug in his lair, the hibernating bear will decide from one day to the next whether to stir himself, a decision generally resting on how hungry he is. While most people are busy making pancakes on Shrove Tuesday, the bear is asking himself, 'To move, or not to move?', quite unaware that his behaviour may have a bearing on man's fate. When he does eventually leave his cave, he will examine the sky and deliver a verdict: according to folk wisdom, if he goes back into his cave, winter will last for another forty days, but if he remains outside, it means that spring has arrived.

Top: *From 'The Bear who Lost a Paw', the Russian folk tale.* Bottom: *The bear as seducer of young girls.* Left: *The bear as man's double,* c. *1940, wearing a masterpiece of tailoring from the 1910s.* Following page: *Drawing by T. Lévigne, 1882, an advertisement for whalebone corsets, showing the early media appeal of bears.*

Bears who Think They are Human

The heroes of Dino Buzatti's *The Famous Invasion of Sicily by Bears* try to imitate men – with disastrous consequences. As they slowly lose their animal characteristics, their behaviour alters and the group is overcome by decadence and degradation. Some bears, however, have coped remarkably well when placed amongst men. The most celebrated literary bears seem even to have *gained* a great deal from their humanization, becoming internationally famous – miniature ambassadors for their countries in some respects. We are all very nationalistic when it comes to bears. Winnie-the-Pooh and Rupert mean as much to the British public as Gros Nounours does to the French; in many ways they are all symbols of a shared, and universally recognized heritage. Though their

ST. MARYS PUBLIC LIBRARY
100 HERB BAUER DR.
ST. MARYS, GEORGIA 31558

BUSCS A L'OURS
BRÉVETÉS S.G.D.G
les Seuls Garantis
INCASSABLES
ET
INDÉCROCHETABLES
33 SOUPLE
32 SOUPLE
31 SOUPLE
30 SOUPLE
29 SOUPLE
33 FORT
32 FORT
31 FORT
30 FORT
29 FORT
33 FORT
32 FORT
31 FORT
30 FORT
29 FORT
31 TRES FORT
30 TRES FORT
29 TRES FORT
C.M.F.A 01245
BUSCS à L'OURS
C.M.F.A 01246
C.M.F.A 01247
BUSCS à L'OURS
BUSCS

MARQUE DE FABRIQUE
DÉPOSÉE
DÉPOSÉE
29 SOUPLE
30 SOUPLE
31 SOUPLE
32 SOUPLE
33 SOUPLE
34 SOUPLE
29 FORT
30 FORT
31 FORT
32 FORT
33 FORT
34 FORT
29 FORT
30 FORT
31 FORT
32 FORT
33 FORT
34 FORT
29 TRES FORT
33 FORT
34 FORT
33 TRES FORT
34 TRES FORT
L'OURS

physical appearance may sometimes cause amusement, it is not an overstatement to describe some of these famous bears as 'stars'. Because the admiration surrounding them is based on a process which simultaneously involves and distances the admirer, providing such endless pleasure, they can lay claim to possessing the very essence of stardom.

The bear – hero of books and films – is, at one and the same time, the child's double, while still essentially remaining a bear. His animal characteristics allow us to look at everyday human experience from a more dispassionate perspective. Despite the fact that Winnie-the-Pooh and Baloo behave as if they were human, we none the less still see them primarily as bears (their fur being the one unchanging sign through which we recognize the beast) who are facing up to their human destiny. Most of them spend their lives in an idyllic world of harmony and tranquillity which would, if it were populated only by human characters, run the risk of descending into dull and limp sentimentality. But these bears inhabit their world as stars and it must be because they are responding to some deep-seated need within us for an ideal being with whom we can identify and in whom we can recognize aspects of our own characters. The bear allows the child at play to sublimate everyday life without losing contact with reality. This perhaps explains why such bears are always depicted upright, a position from which they can view the world from a human perspective, not one of them moving around on all four paws. That in turn is why the real, wild bear in the circus becomes a star by standing on his hind legs: he is transcending his animal origins and challenging the world of mankind.

Left: *Baloo, hero of 'The Jungle Book'. The costume was manufactured by Steiff after a design by Walt Disney. Well-known personalities often have their photographs taken wearing it.* Right: *Although stories have often made fun of bears, depicting them as slow and dull witted, they are in fact highly intelligent animals.*

It follows that when a bear adopts the human habit of wearing clothes, it does not strike us as at all odd, or out of place; sometimes a mere detail is sufficient to remove the bear from his own world and place him in ours. There is something entirely appropriate about the tiny red sweater in which Walt Disney dressed Winnie-the-Pooh, and the tight black velvet jacket and little red skirt worn by Prosper, the famous French bear. Could it be that Alain Saint-Ogan, his creator, anticipated the style of the Eighties, when the fashion designer Jean-Paul Gaultier dressed men in skirts? When the few brief outlines of a cartoon are replaced by a full costume, the result is often elaborate and highly colourful. Paddington's clothing is very precisely indicated. He is comfortably kitted out against the rigours of the British climate, and the overall effect is not smart but utilitarian. He seems to be prepared for anything, storms and all, in his duffle coat, sou'wester and wellingtons. Rupert, in contrast, seems to be portrayed as the complete English gentleman in his elegant check trousers and matching scarf.

Whatever our hero's appearance, from a psychological point of view we

Ah! Ah! je suis vainqueur.

primarily think of him as a human being – which is why children can see him as a friend and feel involved in his fate. Whether his adventures are remotely plausible like Paddington's, or fantastic like Michka's, whether the situations in which he finds himself are ordinary or remarkable, the bear only needs to display all the signs of human fallibility in order to capture a child's imagination. Apparently children do not find anything disconcertingly contradictory in the fact that an animal possesses human characteristics; they simply take the bears to their hearts without a second thought.

The Bear as Superstar

Certain bears have become old and trusted favourites, immortalized on paper in picture books, strip cartoons, story books and tales of adventure. This generation of bears was born before the 1950s, before the growing attractions of the cinema and television took over, to some extent, from words and drawings. These famous bears have enjoyed illustrious careers, and many are still widely known and loved.

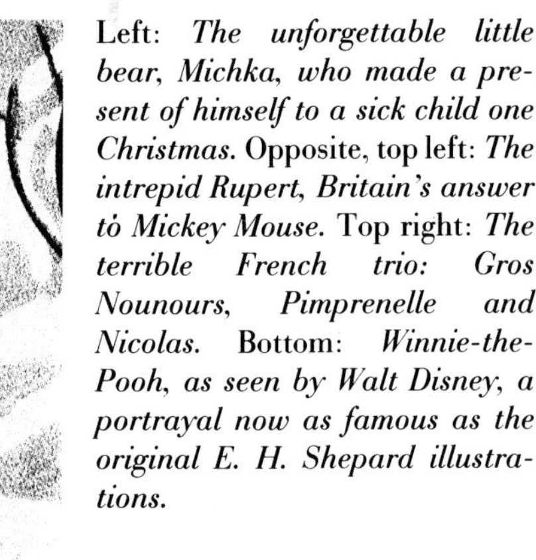

Left: *The unforgettable little bear, Michka, who made a present of himself to a sick child one Christmas.* Opposite, top left: *The intrepid Rupert, Britain's answer to Mickey Mouse.* Top right: *The terrible French trio: Gros Nounours, Pimprenelle and Nicolas.* Bottom: *Winnie-the-Pooh, as seen by Walt Disney, a portrayal now as famous as the original E. H. Shepard illustrations.*

Michka is a hero in Russian folk tales. Many stuffed bears have been named after him, just as many have been called 'Teddy', after King Edward VII or President Roosevelt. He also starred as the mascot for the Moscow Olympics in 1980, but for most people he will always be the unforgettable little bear created in 1941 by Marie Colmont in the Père Castor albums. Michka is a toy who comes to life one Christmas Eve. He takes to the hills, justifying his actions by proclaiming, 'Well, after all I *am* a bear.' Yet, having rediscovered the fun of such freedom, he decides to return to the poor, sick little boy he left behind, and finds that being needed as a companion brings him even greater joy. Without moralizing or indulging in sentimentality, the story of Michka is a lesson in selflessness, inspired by a belief in a better world.

Long before his immortalization by Walt Disney, Baloo had entertained generations of adults and children in Rudyard Kipling's *The Jungle Book*. He plays a part whose character is complemented by his reassuring size and playful face; with his great fat tummy – like an enormous white cushion ideal for cuddling or bouncing up and down on – jolly, easy-going Baloo is full of energy, humour and a love of life, with a weakness for parties and dancing. At the same time, however, he has a strong sense of duty and doing right. Walt Disney may have taken a number of liberties with Kipling's Baloo, who is a far more serious-minded and thoughtful bear, but his creation none the less remains the guardian, adviser and friend of the young man-cub, Mowgli.

First featured in the pages of *The Daily Express* in 1920, Rupert has remained famous ever since. During his long career he has failed only twice to

THE
RUPERT
BOOK
THE
DAILY EXPRESS
ANNUAL

MIEL

MIEL

Top: *Clothing conceals the bear's androgynous form: the ALFA bears of 1950 came close to resembling dolls.* Bottom: *Bears in rudimentary dress, 1950.* Right: *Home-made bears. As the number of bears increases so novelty becomes an all-important factor.*

put in an appearance: once on the death of a Pope, and another on the occasion of a wartime speech by Winston Churchill. Over the years, the cartoon has been drawn by a number of artists and the books of his adventures are always in print. Rupert has also become a national and international star – perhaps he is Britain's answer to Mickey Mouse. As Rupert's fame has spread, the strip cartoon has been translated into eighteen languages. He was created by Mary Tourtel whose own character had a strong influence on the character she chose to give her surrogate son. She was herself an adventurer and pioneering aviator who broke a number of speed records. In this respect she shared Rupert's strong personality. Whatever situations Rupert encounters, this inherited fortitude allows him to be as much at home in the everyday world as in a fairy-tale fantasy land. His bear-like qualities are limited to his head and ears; the hands which peep out from his elegant attire, and the rest of his body are distinctly human. Rupert's popularity has inspired the manufacture of a whole stream of products surrounding both the character and his world. More recently, he has been adapted for a television series, which has proved as successful as the original strip cartoon.

Top: *Winnie-the-Pooh, as immortalized by E. H. Shepard.* Bottom: *Christopher Robin Milne and Pooh, whose close relationship inspired A. A. Milne to record their adventures.* Left: *Saint-Ogan's Prosper, the white bear who first appeared in 'Le Matin' in 1933. Contrasting plush fabric and papier mâché.*

Winnie-the-Pooh is the superstar among bears. His birth was the result of a strange partnership. Christopher Robin Milne's relationship with his teddy bear was particularly close, and the two would often be seen deep in imaginary conversation. No great respecter of rules and social niceties, Pooh – according to Christopher Robin – had a great talent for telling wild and wonderful stories. Christopher Robin's father, Alexander Milne (a columnist on *Punch*), became fascinated by his son's intimacy with his teddy bear and hit upon the idea of writing about the adventures of Winnie-the-Pooh: he knew that he had only to sit quietly next to them in order to capture the wanderings of his child's imagination. However, Christopher Robin was brought up at a time and in a social milieu when a child's early years were spent in a nursery, and so it was actually Mrs Milne who took on the delicate task of relaying her son's tales to her husband. It was she who collected the spontaneous ramblings which poured forth from her son's imagination, and passed on this raw material to be refined by her husband. In later years Christopher Robin recalled how many of the passages in his father's books described in detail those games and adventures he had indeed shared with his teddy bear. As a strange coda to this story, in 1952 Christopher Robin published an article in which he revealed that his father disliked children; that, as a child, he had scarcely ever seen his father, and that it was actually his nanny who had read him his father's stories, even after they were published.

It is at this stage that a fifth person, who was to prove decisive for the future of Winnie-the-Pooh, appears on the scene. This was E. H. Shepard, whose drawings were forever to immortalize the adventures of the young boy and his thoughtful companion. In the legend surrounding the birth of Winnie-the-Pooh, one aspect remains a mystery: whether it was Christopher Robin's bear which had inspired Shepard or the teddy belonging to his own son, Graham? The bear in the pictures is not, sadly, the same bear as the one owned by the

boy who inspired the tales (a discrepancy which cannot be fully explained). Shepard's illustrations have been frequently copied. Walt Disney's full-length cartoon, *Winnie-the-Pooh and the Honey Tree*, issued in 1960, was at first coldly received, but such a reaction was only to be expected when the appearance of a figure so familiar from the drawings in the books was in any way changed. The film's subsequent success has meant, however, that Hollywood's Winnie-the-Pooh has to some extent overshadowed Shepard's creation.

More significantly, though, manufacturers of stuffed bears seem to have used the original illustrations as a model for their designs. Since 1930 various imitation Winnie-the-Poohs – all quite different from the more traditionally shaped teddy bear – have been enormously successful. It is certainly the case that this dumpy little bear, whose shape has all the signs of an all-too-healthy appetite and who was captured so perfectly in Shepard's illustrations, marked an important turning-point in the evolution of the teddy bear's design.

Winnie-the-Pooh's qualities – his good sense, his initiative and his knack of doing the right thing at the right time – would be a credit to most humans. He is portrayed as a thoroughly nice being, whose generous character and modest outlook are quite unblemished. Not surprisingly he has had a fanatical following, and has inspired a large number of clubs, societies, conventions, festivals, books, toys and sweets.

A makeshift bear dating from c. *1940 made out of roughly cut cotton pieces, with glass eyes, rudimentary stitching, a clothed tartan body and exterior jointing – a perfect example of how teddy bears, although often inexpensive, are still objects of great affection.*

Prosper was the brain-child of Alain Saint-Ogan, the modern French comic strip's inventor. Though he probably owes his fame to *Zig et Puce*, this creator of magical creatures always had a soft spot for the bear. Prosper was a white bear who was first brought to public attention in *Le Matin*, in a daily strip first published in 1933. Its polar setting meant that the strip broke new ground, not falling foul of the clichés which inevitably surround stories of brown bears. A tiny pot-bellied beast with skinny limbs, only Prosper's ears and his long snout betray his genealogical origins. Like so many other bears, Prosper had an unfortunate brush with the world of men and he still carries the scar of this misfortune, forever condemned to have a chain hanging from his nose. Returning as a convict to his old life, Prosper may remind us of Jean Valjean in Victor Hugo's *Les Misérables*, though his tale is not as exemplary, nor famous, as that of his prototype, for it largely consists of a long series of wonderfully absurd adventures.

Saint-Ogan had first-hand experience of the discrepancy between the behaviour of real animals and our anthropomorphic conception of them. He was filming some cinema newsreel in a zoo one day when he was attacked by a bear. It was only thanks to a dozen keepers and policemen that he escaped with nothing but a torn pair of trousers. When he came to create Prosper, popular fiction and reality met halfway: the little bear is a grumpy and irritable character, easily riled and sometimes even violent, with little sense of humour . . . but he is still likeable. The fact that life is not always easy for the little chap strengthens his defence in this respect; the unflinching accuracy of Saint-Ogan's description of the cruel environment lends weight to our sympathy for little Prosper.

Certain other bears have risen to stardom remarkably quickly, as books have become merely one aspect of the post-war media explosion. This new generation of bears have achieved fame in a variety of fields, on the radio and television with special series, in films and through advertising. Despite their success, their popularity may well prove short lived, because, as children grow up they become increasingly aware, demanding and capricious, and their likes and dislikes become increasingly unpredictable. Rather than passively following trends, they can, and frequently do, assert their own tastes, influencing fashion sometimes to the point of actually changing its course. These stars are also, of course, now confronted by a much greater choice. But they are all the more vulnerable; they would do well to savour their moment of glory, which may prove to be a brief one.

Dressing up a bear often affords him protection rather than simply entertaining the child. Here, only the head is in its original 1920 state; the limbs have been completely remade out of old stockings, while a baby's cardigan helps to keep the arms in place.

In 1983 the market was invaded by the Care Bears, who illustrate how the teddy bear's personality has fragmented. The beasts are available in a wide range of sizes and materials; they are the colour of chewing gum; an embroidered label is emblazoned on their bellies, indicating their character or mood; and a small tuft of fur sticks up between their ears. The poor bear is apparently no longer capable of satisfying his owner's demands in his own right – his emotional range is just too limited – and bears especially raised solely for this caring function seem to have made the old-style teddy bears almost redundant. It is perfectly fitting that such an unearthly collection of bears should permanently inhabit a bank of clouds amongst the rainbows.

The story of Paddington Bear's origins seems like a fairy-tale. It was while Michael Bond was searching for a last-minute Christmas present that he saw a bear sitting all alone on a shelf in Selfridge's department store and felt inspired to create the character with whom we are now all so familiar. His story begins in 1956 at Paddington underground station, where we find him wearing a large pair of wellington boots, waiting, and watching the crowds go by. The label hanging from his coat reads 'Please look after this bear. Thank you'. This rather pathetic sight tugs at the reader's heartstrings, and further investigation reveals that Paddington's situation is indeed a tangled one. Though his duffle coat and a love of marmalade make him quintessentially English, Paddington actually comes from Peru. We learn that his Aunt Lucie has remained closer to her Peruvian roots and still wears clothes which recall her origins; it is *she* who acts as a constant reminder of the very different culture from which Paddington has come, for he never mentions it. The only thing which emphasises Paddington's peripatetic status is the fact that he is never without his suitcase. Paddington is a successful combination of a grown-up's mature sense of independence and a child-like purity and innocence. Proof of the success and undoubted appeal of this formula is the endless stream of products inspired by Paddington, which shows no signs of drying up.

While English children have had Rupert, Winnie-the-Pooh and Paddington, children in other countries have been enchanted by other, no less popular, bears. For French children growing up during the Sixties, Gros Nounours is unforgettable. Born in 1960, this star of the small screen was based on an

English television character called Teddy, who first appeared in 1951 in the company of a little clown, Andy Pandy, and whose career stretched over thirty years. Although Teddy's French counterpart – featured with the Sandman and his three nephews – was already paying nightly visits to see his friends Pimprenelle and Nicolas in the early Fifties, it was only in 1962 that this fantasy world took on its own definitive identity, when the affectionate little hero swapped his originally rather harsh name of Gros Ours for a more friendly one. Paul Laydu, who created Gros Nounours and the characters around him, started broadcasting *Bonne Nuit les Petits*. This programme, using television fantasy as a way of encouraging obedience, developed out of the simple idea of devising a way of getting children into bed. The warm-hearted Gros Nounours willingly accepted the challenge of reconciling fairy-tales with the new imagery of the space age. He drove around on a cloud as if it were a space shuttle, accompanied by the Sandman, whose shower of gold sent children off into the arms of Morpheus. The little bear became a sort of Father Christmas; he entered people's homes through the window, told his jokes and stories, and sent children off to bed to dream happily ever after.

Little boys used to be denied the pleasure of dressing up dolls, but the teddy bear, appealing to boys and girls alike, filled the gap. A mother obviously helped out with this specimen from the 1940s; his shape is rather unorthodox.

Nounours's popularity was prolonged, with some thousand episodes to his credit. He even made the headlines, as is proved by one newspaper article of January 1965: 'Nounours, Rocambole and De Gaulle, All Stars of the Small Screen'. He could not be accused of being just a dumb little beast with an insipid voice, or merely an effective means of helping out exhausted parents incapable of persuading their children to go to bed. He inspired a tidal wave of thousands of products featuring both him and his little friends. Although these were all manufactured under licence from the TV station RTF, everyone jumped onto the Gros Nounours bandwagon: eight hundred thousand records were produced, seven million postcards and an avalanche of toys. His success was seemingly a God-sent opportunity for teddy bear manufacturers, whose sales tripled in 1962 alone. Unfortunately, his successor, Colargol, did not enjoy the same success. In 1983 the magazine *Télé 7 jours* mounted a campaign to have Nounours returned to the screen, a move supported by sixty-five per cent of the French population . . . but legends cannot be so easily revived.

The Dress Makes the Bear

Thanks to the efforts of children and manufacturers, bears have become increasingly 'human'; a whole wardrobe has been created for them ranging from stockings and suspenders to alpine *Lederhosen*.

Dressing up dolls has always been considered a female occupation from which little boys have generally been excluded. The toy industry recognized and catered for this discrepancy by giving boys a series of human-like heroes, complete with jointed limbs, muscles and military-style uniforms. The teddy bear, on the other hand, is not exclusive to either boys or girls: with his asexual and androgynous appearance, everyone can enjoy playing with him. Although not many people make teddy bears at home, the same is not true of their

clothes. These improvised outfits range from borrowed dolls' outfits and recycled baby clothes to a child's early, halting attempts at needlework. Toy manufacturers have made their own contribution to the development of an ursine 'look'. The bear's coloured coat has changed according to fashion: from the two-tone clown bears of the 1940s to the present-day pastel-coloured versions, bears have always had a sense of style.

As early as 1908 Steiff introduced an 'animal doll', complete with its own wardrobe. Today, these fashionable bears, in their sailor suits and morning coats, vie with each other as if for a 'best-dressed' prize, but are, however, more often collected than played with. The French ALFA range was innovatory in this respect: as early as 1935, they decided to dress their bears in skirts, underclothes and polka-dot jackets in various colours, while more recently, Boulgom – another manufacturer – has produced a range of simple clothes for bears. These contrast sharply with the excesses of those anonymous designers employed by manufacturers to dress thousands of bears; sometimes their tastelessness knows no bounds. Overwhelmed by mountains of material and lace, buried beneath hats and feathers, forced into tightly cut costumes, these poor long-suffering bears smile resolutely, no doubt wishing for the designer clothes sported by their smarter companions.

First steps in knitting worn by a 1940s bear, a stylistic tour de force. As the teddy bear gradually changed in shape, the bear's limbs became shorter and stockier and they became increasingly difficult to dress.

Bears who Pretend to be Human

Somewhere between animal and object, capable of movement and with the appearance of an animal, the mechanical bear, like many of his literary counterparts, has human characteristics. During the nineteenth century the mechanical bear, or automaton, was generally a 'one-off' creation made to be admired in the drawing room. Clothed in authentic fur, he was astonishingly realistic. He was later eclipsed by a cheaper mass-produced model, which was intended to be played with rather than simply looked at. In appearance these toys still emphasized the bear's animal characteristics and seemed perfectly authentic. They reached a peak of popularity in the 1950s and 1960s, when production was dominated by the Japanese. Today the enthusiasm for such toys has diminished, as has their output, and they have been replaced by bears made of plastic and lightly covered in brown fur fabric.

Mechanical bears do not possess the often threatening or annoying qualities of other robotic toys. Rather than seeming to hold a distorting mirror before us or being maddeningly repetitive, they comment on man's social foibles by acting out the daily rituals of family life, work or leisure. From the shoe-shine bear to the executive bear seated at his desk, they present reality, underlined with humour.

Some bears conceal a highly sophisticated mechanism beneath their fur exterior. The Schuco bear, manufactured during the 1920s, is perhaps the ancestor of them all: by moving his tail he would say yes or no (a requirement which, after all, is essential to an independent existence!). In the last ten years a series of innovations have turned stuffed bears into semi-human clones.

Manufactured by the industrial equivalents of Dr Frankenstein, who have been spurred on by a desire for complete authenticity, bears have been produced whose hearts beat, thus fulfilling man's age-old dream of giving life to inanimate objects. Gradually, step by step, the bear comes closer to man.

In the beginning was the word. The bear was deprived of speech, however, though for good reason: he was all ears and made a very good listener. But, if speech was the only thing the teddy bear lacked, he has quickly made up for it. Over the last two years a vociferous army of bears has suddenly appeared. After listening quietly for decades, they consequently had a great deal to get off their chests! Conversation is no longer one-sided as bears have at last been given the power of speech. Their snouts quiver, their bottom jaws move and words pour forth. The greatest linguistic exhibitionists are actually little more than furry cassette recorders who are always ready to talk about their life and adventures (even the more inhibited ones seem cleverer than their appearance would have one believe). Their secret is a microchip with a 400-word vocabulary which can be mixed up in any number of combinations. As a result their remarks can often take a playful and unexpected turn, and then they sound more like Professor Brainstorm.

A Japanese automaton, manufactured at the height of the vogue for mechanical bears in 1950. Often humorous, these bears imitate aspects of our day-to-day existence. As the label suggests, when this boss starts to write, his sheet of paper remains blank.

When turned upside down or shaken, the earliest teddy bears used to emit an odd grunting noise, sounding more like a cow than a bear. Their more modern equivalents, however, cover a far more sophisticated register; in America, there are even bears capable of reproducing the soothing sounds of the pre-natal world, furry Orpheuses for babes-in-arms. Hospital tests carried out on infants between one and sixteen weeks old have proved the calming influence of this type of bear, who eases the child's transition from the womb to the outside world.

Talking bears are not just for children – adults too seem all the more attentive to a bear with the power of speech, as is demonstrated by an incident that took place not in the realm of fantasy and adventure, but in the very real, cut-throat world of commerce. On this occasion, two sorts of bear were distributed to the participants at a conference in the United States. Those given to the men were dressed in a pin-striped suit, white shirt and red tie and, when activated, said in a deep voice: 'You are on the path to success, you're a born winner.' Women were given bears dressed in a white suit with a striped red blouse, and which gently murmured: 'Be what you want to be. You're perfect, absolutely perfect. Mister bear says you're a winner.' By answering the questions we never dare ask, these assembly-line prototypes, despite their demagogical overtones, seem to have satisfied some hidden need because over half a million of them have since been sold.

Goldilocks and the Three Bears

In the fairy-tale *Goldilocks and the Three Bears* we are presented with a group of bears whose behaviour is so like that of humans that the story could almost be renamed *Goldilocks and the Little Family*. This has not always been the

I AM THE BOSS
I MAY LOOK BUSY
BUT I'M ONLY CONFUSED!

case, however, and the protagonists in the earliest versions of the story are *all* animals. The tale is Scottish in origin and tells of the disruption of the three bears' little world by a vixen. In Eleanor Muir's 1831 version, *The Celebrated Nursery Tale of the Three Bears*, though the story's outline remains the same, the vixen is replaced by an old lady: the bears behave like vicious wild animals and get rid of her in a particularly barbaric fashion. On finding her asleep, they start to chase her in frantic 'cops-and-robbers' fashion and attempt, as only old-fashioned bears know how, to throw her onto a fire, before trying to drown her. The old lady turns out to be pretty hard-skinned, but the bears eventually get the better of her by throwing her from a church steeple and, finally, by eating her. One can only hope that any little child given the story as a birthday present did not take the events too seriously, since the work's realism leaves nothing to the imagination.

It was Robert Southey's book, *The Doctor*, of 1837, which introduced a less terrifying and brutal end to the story. In his version the intruder escapes through the window and nobody knows what has become of her, her departure being as mysterious as her arrival (this is still a feature of the Goldilocks story). In 1856 another, more mildly disposed gentleman, Joseph Cundall, transformed the intruder into a young girl, though her name, Silver Hair, still recalls the old lady in earlier versions of the tale. In 1889 the curls took on their golden hue and by 1904 the story arrived at the definitive form we now know as *Goldilocks and the Three Bears*. As the elements in the story have become more or less invariable, so it has provided a wonderful stylistic challenge to illustrators. Like painters of sacred subjects whose talent lies in interpretative ability rather than narrative invention, so illustrators of this tale have delighted in giving a new slant to the portrayal of the mischievous little girl and the well-known routine of the three bears.

Even in the versions where the three bears treat their intruder somewhat harshly, they are still shown as living like human beings – with their little

house, their little family and their daily afternoon walks. Yet, this naïve depiction of family life and daily routine scarcely paints a flattering picture of human existence. Though Daddy Bear, Mummy Bear and Baby Bear seem to epitomize the perfect nuclear family in their neat and tidy little house, they do appear rather eccentric, each insistent on having his or her own particular dish, bed and chair. It is a world where each member of the family knows his or her proper place, Mummy Bear's chair is not too big, Daddy Bear's is not too small; everything is designed to match its owner's identity. In this closed world from which incongruity or excess have been banished, everything is in its place and there is a place for everything, a law which extends from objects to individuals.

Since 1831 there have been numerous different versions of 'Goldilocks and The Three Bears', a story in which the bears act like humans. In this French version of 1900 Goldilocks is significantly called 'Touche-à-tout' (Nosey Parker).

Everybody has a place and a part to play – and is happy with it. Each member of this anonymous family is well integrated into the whole: Mummy Bear seems content with her domestic role, while Daddy Bear is the epitome of manhood in the same way that Baby Bear embodies childhood. Finicky they certainly are, and their outlook narrow minded. When they go for a walk in the forest, tea is not only waiting for them when they return, it is already served. . . . Their pleasures are healthy and regulated and nothing is left to chance. It is not really very surprising, then, that there is no place for an outsider in this rigid routine; spontaneity and disorder would be threatening to their existence. Although their diet has changed since 1831, porridge and chocolate having replaced old ladies, the encouraging improvement in their behaviour still has some way to go before their human characteristics are matched by humane values.

Bursting into this haven of peace and order, Goldilocks's presence seems intolerable. The house is thrown into chaos and the family unit is placed in jeopardy. The violation of their privacy and possessions echoes through Mummy Bear's and Baby Bear's sobs and Daddy Bear's anger, each reacting according to type: 'Who's been eating in my bowl?', 'Who's been sitting in my chair?', 'Who's been sleeping in my bed?' Goldilocks, however, has not stolen anything – she has merely come to look around, try things out and explore a bit. Is it the act of trespassing that the bears find intolerable, or is it rather that they resent this stranger's intrusive gaze, seeing it as a form of voyeurism violating their private life? When Goldilocks escapes, they resume their normal routine without any sign of remorse or belated generosity. Totally unconcerned, in their selfishness and indifference, about the fate of a young girl all alone in the forest, they chase her away. The questions that the reader might ask himself – did she visit the house out of curiosity or was she in urgent need of refuge? – do not even occur to the bears. Goldilocks's haste in eating and going to sleep suggests, perhaps, that she has already travelled a long distance and still has a long way to go. The story does not elaborate, and as the bears are quite unconcerned about where she might have come from, where she is going bothers them even less. Her departure comes as a relief – what they most hate is disruption of their routine – and, as far as they are concerned, that is the end of the story. Sadly, this family has little to recommend it. With its inward-looking structure, its hostility to outsiders, its pathetic rituals and its obsession with order and punctuality, it represents human values at their least attractive.

In 1976 Henriette Bichonnier attempted to give the tale a more attractive ending, while remaining faithful to the socio-cultural context of the original: confronted with the mess Goldilocks has caused, Goldilocks's mother invites Baby Bear to do the same thing in her own house, thus teaching him the joys of curiosity – and the excitement of disorder – which he has been denied at home. This is a human initiative, however, and the bears themselves remain as ponderous as ever. Psychoanalytic investigation has also taken up the case of these three rather dull bears; Bruno Bettelheim identifies them with the Oedipal triangle. Here they serve merely as the catalysts for the difficult but decisive choice that Goldilocks – or every child – must make. Confronted with the three identities of Father, Mother and Child, the young girl is unsure whether she wants to share the safety of Daddy Bear's bed, the comfort of Mummy Bear's bed, or, as she is denied the possibility of remaining a baby, simply to become herself. It seems clear that humanization, whether it is immediate or the outcome of a search, is not something that bears accomplish with particular success. Though certainly oblivious to the fate of Buzatti's bears in Sicily, the three bears do not make a great success of their transformation into humans.

A Schuco bear of 1920. He has boot-button eyes and paws recovered in velvet, and when his tail is turned, he nods or shakes his head. This was a revolutionary model and is the ancestor of today's technologically sophisticated bears.

THE BEAR AND HIS OWNER

Left: *A photograph taken in 1924. The bear is almost as big as the child, who is obviously enjoying being photographed amongst his toys.* Right: *By 1928 the child and the bear have grown up together. Only the bear's ears have changed; they are perpetually bent forward now from hearing so many secrets.* Previous page: *The little bear tamer, 1900. The wild bear's appearance has little in common with the more familiar teddy bear.*

Very soon after a child is born, his teddy bear arrives – unless, of course, it is already there and waiting. A baby is not entirely oblivious to his bedfellow, although he is largely preoccupied with his more immediate needs for food and warmth. Less sleepy and unresponsive than one might think, a baby is in fact highly sensitive as regards things tactile. We would be wrong to think that he is not taking any notice of the soft, cuddly object by his side, for this little being's life seems to depend on one essential need – the desire for contact with others. While the new-born child may appear to possess more highly developed faculties than perhaps he actually does, he has no notion that this new companion is anything more than transitory. He cannot be expected to understand that the bear will be staying with him, remaining close by and destined to become a firm friend, because at this stage he is incapable of emotional projection.

It is easy to understand why there is so much competition surrounding the giving of a teddy bear to a child. Everybody wants to initiate or be part of this lifelong friendship. According to a study carried out in France, it is mainly grandparents who want to proffer a sign of their love in the form of a teddy bear – like benevolent fairies bestowing good wishes for the future. By acknowledging thus the existence of the new-born child the grandparents are likely to prolong their own lives. Often, the child is overwhelmed with stuffed toys, surrounded by as many as half a dozen in the first year of his life. As soon as the child is old enough to exercise some choice in the matter, he decides which one is to be his favourite. This is apparently an arbitrary process which anyone else is powerless to influence; the child's judgement is final. Habitually, it is the teddy bear who proves to be most popular, condemning the losers to oblivion. Selected by one child in every two, Teddy wins hands down in the favourite toy stakes.

Left: *The bear as man's friend, the role he plays best.* Right: *The constant creation of new materials ensures that the demand for softer, more sensual and cuddly coats can always be satisfied. This bear was made by Boulgom. It illustrates how the bear's size should allow the child to hold it comfortably.*

It is all-important that this first bear – and there will be more to follow, no doubt – is the right size for its owner. If the bear is too big or too unwieldly he must be discarded, for however soft or furry he might be, his body must be the right scale to allow his owner to cuddle him easily.

Not only is the bear the recipient of the child's first murmurs and gurgles, more importantly he also carries the smells by which the child gets his bearings during his first few traumatic months in the world. Of the five senses with which the newborn child is endowed, the sense of smell is the most developed: within the first few days of his existence he discovers in his bear, carrying the scent of his mother's body, a reassuring, undemanding companion. With our modern obsession with hygiene, we have come to overlook this crucial role and regularly consign teddy bears to the washing

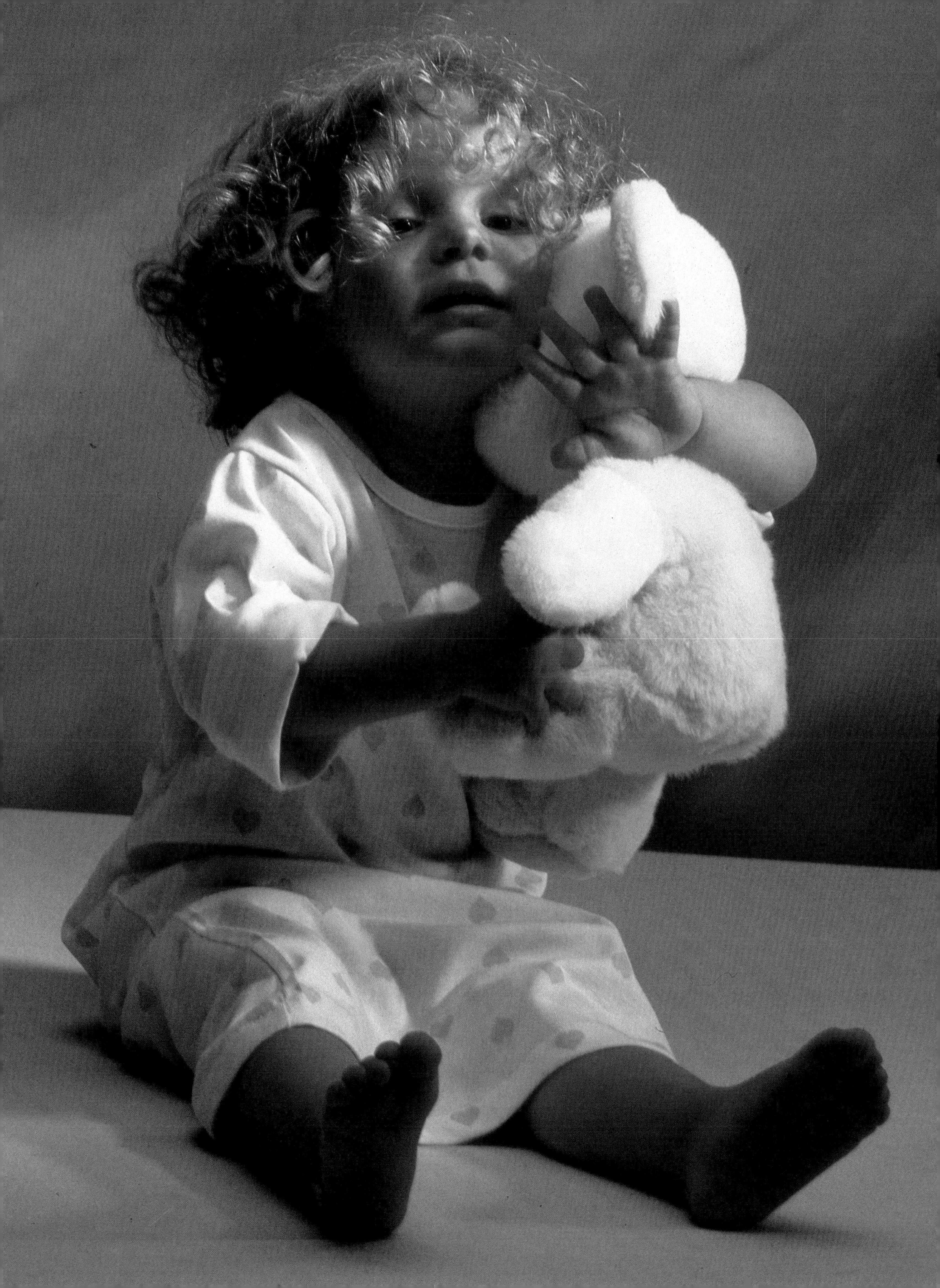

machine, thus confusing and threatening to destroy the important relationship the child has established with the toy. It seems paradoxical – even ridiculous – that at a time when child psychology has gained such widespread recognition, we nevertheless go out of our way to manufacture bears whose main selling-point is that they are easily washable. The teddy bear is also responsible for developing the child's other senses, the first signs of pleasure and excitement being provoked by the feel of the bear's soft, silky, furry coat. Sucked, stroked and cuddled, the teddy bear is the object of a child's first tender courtship.

Top: *A picture taken in 1956. It is obvious that a child's first bear provides a focus for its need for affection.* Bottom: *A photograph sent to a father fighting on the front line in 1939 to let him know that Teddy is in good health.* Left: *Playing with a teddy bear allows the child to create a world of its own; he can treat the bear–child just as he wishes.*

The teddy bear becomes the first object to give the child unalloyed pleasure, free from ambiguity or disappointment: it is a classic case of possessive love. When the child becomes more outgoing and grows a little stronger, he is able to protect his property and is even capable of fighting over the bear. If the teddy bear goes missing, a family S.O.S. is issued, and tension, upset and emotion reign until he is rediscovered. As the child's guardian angel, there is never any necessity to make excuses for a teddy bear: he can be taken anywhere without explanation. The teddy bear protects the child, freeing him from anxieties and helping him to overcome his fear of the unknown, especially at night-time – perhaps the most disturbing aspect of the frightening world outside. When the child is taken out of the family environment, it is his teddy bear who acts as a mother substitute in the face of the terrors of an unknown world. Though a visit to the hospital is the most obvious instance, any trip outside the secure family home can prove traumatic and it is not uncommon to find a teddy bear packed away in a suitcase or satchel during a summer trip. All of these qualities make the teddy bear into what the English psychoanalyst Winnicott has described as a 'transitional object', the importance of which is universally recognized.

As the child grows up, so his teddy bear – be it a childhood bear or one more recently acquired – grows with him. Whether or not they grow up together, the nature of the relationship develops and assumes different characteristics. The bear is an extremely adaptable partner, noted for his versatility. He is the means by which the child makes contact with others; given, loaned and returned, he becomes a mediator in exchanges both with adults and other children. The teddy bear is the ideal companion in stimulating children's play, allowing his owners to externalize their conflicts and pleasures through a character who is an exten-

sion of themselves while simultaneously retaining his own distinct personality. He plays a part in the creation of a private world where the bear (a mere 'extension' of his owner) can be treated at will by his alter ego, in defiance of the interdictions of authority. He presents the child with the opportunity, like Alice, of going through the looking-glass, of escaping from the adult world and entering a sphere where all order has been reversed and where the child himself makes the decisions. A teddy bear will participate in the most varied of games, share the wildest stories and accept Fate's bitterest blows; whether active or passive, servile or sublime, he is by turn an accomplice and an outlet for emotions.

With such a degree of close contact, the bear may well – indeed almost

Left: *The bear is the child's double; he shares all his adventures and experiences. The child tells the bear everything and the bear willingly takes part in the game.* Right: *The bear is an ambiguous friend, whose expected comfort and protection may prove equivocal!*

certainly will – take a few hard knocks, as the child's curiosity over his internal workings results in periodic medical and surgical experiments. These leave a legacy of scars and amputations which merely add to the teddy bear's value. Yet he is the best and most forgiving of friends, in whom the child can confide and to whom he can confess his fears and disappointments without anything being demanded in return. He is the world's best listener. . . . Hi-tech bears, with their heart transplants and eternal babble, repudiate these traditions as they overstep the role of the silent companion with impunity.

The bear is, of course, most in demand, just like all best friends, when things are not going well. In times of illness, it is often a teddy bear who has the first taste of the medicine and tries out the injections. And when things are going very badly, he can be a real life-saver. Hospitalization is one of the most unnerving experiences a child has to confront and on these occasions his teddy bear acts as a refuge, offering help and protection. The American group,

"... shadows tonight
Have struck more terror to the soul of Richard
Than can the substance of ten thousand soldiers"
KING RICHARD III
AT THIS
VERY MOMENT
"EVEREADY"
FLASHLIGHTS
IN
TEN THOUSAND
HANDS
ARE
BLOTTING OUT
TEN THOUSAND
SHADOWS
No 950
EVEREADY
EXTRA LONG LIFE BATTERY
NATIONAL CARBON CO.
"EVEREADY"
FLASHLIGHTS &
fresh BATTERIES
ATIONAL CARBON COMPANY, INC.
of Union Carbide UCC & Carbon Corp

070

Pediatric Projects Inc., keeps a large collection of bears, each one more lame, footsore and poorly than the last: having experienced a wide range of illnesses, these bears offer children suffering from similar misfortunes, a source of comfort and identification. While another's misery is certainly no consolation, it at least allows the child to feel less isolated; the bear increases the child's self-confidence and thus hastens his cure. Russel MacLean began giving bears to children in his Ohio hospital as early as 1951, convinced of the comfort they could provide for his patients. The results were conclusive: doctors, psychiatrists and psychologists all acknowledged the stuffed bear's therapeutic value. As the idea took hold, so it became formalized in 1970 with the establishment of 'Good Bears of the World', an organization which distributed bears to the children of the Boat People in order to help them build a new life and come to terms with their terrible memories. Placing this tiny object in the arms of children who have suffered so much and expecting a mere stuffed toy to be able to help heal their wounds and restore in them some sort of emotional balance seems a tall order, but in a desperate situation like this – where absolutely everything has been lost, including any feeling of identity – this simple yet powerful gift works wonders.

Right: *The infant passes through the mirror of experience as he plays with his bear, acting as parent and child at the same time.* Left: *Stiffly posed in front of a parkland backdrop, there is an extraordinary, timeless gravity in the child's stare.*

Stuffed bears are not always, of course, used to such generous ends – man's Machiavellian nature is ever alert. While some bears are equipped with tape recorders that fascinate children with wondrous tales, and some, stiffened by splints, comfort young patients, others have had their stomachs stuffed with time bombs and have been dropped by parachute. Such is man's nature that he

Bonne Année
DIX
2154/x

1259

Bonne Année
1222

PARIS
650

Bonne Année

Bonne Année
DIX
PARIS
2002

Bonne Année
1233

Right: *Often the bear still has his own place in the adult's bedroom as this 1950 advertisement illustrates.* Left: *The child's favourite plaything joins him on greetings cards – these postcards were published between 1910 and 1930.* Centre: *A bear from 1930, similar to the one in the card by his right ear.*

'The Warm Bedroom of His Childhood'

Here it was, the bedroom where they had chatted together, where he had brought her tea. On the ground was the green dress, the teapot, the two cups, pieces of string, some shoes and the large stuffed bear, lying with its legs in the air. Patrice she had called him. Sometimes, when he had brought her tea, she had had Patrice next to her. She had slept with him. [. . .]

He wandered about all day, shivering in his coat, going up and down stairs, going into the bedrooms, putting on the lights, opening and closing drawers, looking at himself in the mirror so as not to feel alone, switching out the lights, going out, sitting on one of the stairs and glancing through a book. [. . .]

At nine in the evening he went into her room and opened the wardrobe, looked at the dresses hanging there like corpses, leaned forward to breathe in their perfume. [. . .] His foot knocked against the stuffed bear lying on the floor. He picked it up. [. . .]

He went downstairs, holding Patrice by the hand, and went into the bathroom. He put the bear and Papi's book on the white lacquer stool opposite the porcelain washbasin, for company. [. . .]

Once again, he removed the safety catch. Even to die, you had to make a living gesture, press the trigger. [. . .] Yes, that was how it was done, with the barrel against the temple. But not him, his index finger did not want to. He was just trying it out. [. . .] Once, she had winked at him. She winked at him, and his index finger wanted to. 'Go to bed now, it's late,' a voice whispered in his ear as he slowly slumped over. With his head against the stool, between the bear's paws, he entered the warm bedroom of his childhood.

Albert Cohen, *Belle du Seigneur.*

is capable of using a symbol of tenderness to such treacherous ends.

A Phoenix Rising from the Ashes

Childhood passes. During the great upheavals of adolescence, relationships with teddy bears go through a strained and impulsive stage. Resolutely confronting their destiny, adolescents turn their backs on their bears or abandon them altogether – a gesture which symbolizes a belief that childhood has come to an end. They cast aside their old friends, either indifferent to their fate or in the full knowledge that their parents will become their teddy bears' new guardians. As yet inexperienced in the transitory ways of the world, these adolescents scarcely imagine that one day they and their bears may well renew their acquaintance; they do not know how snap decisions are often touchingly reversed. They may well rediscover the charms of their bears, though their attitude towards them will have changed completely. The teddy bear, the 'transitional object', is sometimes ostentatiously displayed in a bedroom, though all too often he is consigned to some neglected corner. Occasionally parents set out to undermine the relationship of child and teddy bear with the odd sarcastic remark, not realizing that in the normal course of events it will end of its own accord. Indeed, the collector Peter Bull has said that his passion for collecting teddy bears was the result of a childhood trauma. Believing that at the age of sixteen her son was far too old to play with toys, his mother stole his bear one day while he was at school, and gave it away. Subsequently, right up until his death, Peter Bull would not leave the house without his two favourite teddy bears, fearing that they too might suffer the same dreadful fate.

Left: *The bear often carries the scars of intimacy; this bear made in 1950 has lost an arm.* Right: *Washing the bear. This is an everyday experience and should not be confused with an obsession with hygiene. It would be harmful to destroy the smell of this transitional object.*

The onset of adulthood provides an ideal moment for fixing an image of childhood in one's mind. The traumas and transformations of adolescence are such that they stimulate a need for some compensatory reference point in which the image of childhood can be invested. The teddy bear often takes on this role, crystallizing memories of the past in a process of rediscovery, a process which can be a necessary form of regression during this psychologically taxing time. In this process, the teddy fulfils the most essential of his many roles as a symbol of emotional attachment; he becomes a constant and reliable source of calm and security. After all, wasn't a certain younger son of a certain queen accused of sleeping with a teddy bear at the foot of his bed, even at the age of twenty-two? This fact was of course seized upon by the media as conclusive proof that the prince was a reticent romantic.

The teddy bear also plays an important part in affairs of the heart. To give somebody a bear – with all the connotations he carries in terms of love and

Bonne Année

For the first ten years of my life, Pierrot has always been at my side, faithful to the end.

Shall I prove it?

Take a violent episode in my life, for example, when my right eye was perforated by the blade of a pair of scissors. He stayed by my side in the hospital for all the long months that were needed for the wound to heal.

I operated on the piece of agate in his right eye after each of the operations on my own eye.

I changed his dressings regularly, every time the nurses came to change mine.

Every time I had eye drops, I gave him some. . . .

Six months later, his head was as damp as a sponge and the straw inside was beginning to rot.

All this was happening at exactly the same time that I was having my last operation – the final attempt to save my eye.

Professor Paufique then advised me about the operation which was necessary to save the bear's head. The nurses helped me, doing everything properly and seriously: his plush coat was cut open, the straw taken out and replaced with fresh cotton, and the eye cavity was sewn back into place.

With the passage of time, my one-eyed Pierrot has nothing more to show than a scar above his eyelid.

Gilbert.

Left: *Bears are given to sick children to help them come to terms with their illness and the treatment they have to undergo.* Top right: *The bear during adolescence.* Bottom right: *Playing seen as confrontation with everyday life.*

friendship – is a clear indication of the strength and permanence of a new relationship. With his role as a 'transitional object' long past, he becomes a mediator, capable of playing a variety of parts: a good luck token carried everywhere by the loved one, he can sit at home enthroned, a symbol of the emotions invested in him, attracting constant attention. As a love token, however, the bear also carries more disturbing connotations. Childhood is that one aspect of a loved one's life which is inaccessible and irrevocably past. By placing a teddy bear in their arms, we secretly hope that by stimulating affection for the bear we will evoke the happy memories of this shadowy and unknown part of their lives that will in turn lead to a greater understanding and a more lasting relationship.

When the moment comes to leave the family home, the teddy bear is either part of the baggage or left behind on the shelf. If left he will probably be consigned to a cellar or an attic, a deposed childhood king bundled away amongst a pile of memories, left to do battle against the dust and the passage of time, trapped between nostalgia and solitude. Otherwise he will languish on his absent owner's bed like the guardian of a deserted temple. If he takes part in the great adventure and joins his owner in his new independent life, his presence is just as likely to be discreet and reserved, as it is to be rather shamelessly ostentatious. Sometimes, he will even continue to share his owner's bed, even though a new partner has been found as substitute 'transitional object'. On the other hand, the young adult may well feel that his *old* companion carries too many childhood associations and decide to buy a new bear – a new bear for a new life. Such teddy bears carry somewhat ironic associations, although this does not prevent them from being relied upon for comfort and security. Indeed, Paddington's creator, Michael Bond, discovered from an opinion poll that the main purchasers of the large version of this stuffed bear were young girls leaving their family to set up home on their own. A charismatic and reassuring figure, Paddington was in this instance acting as a surrogate father.

Top: *In 1905 bears were so popular that a woman would carry one in her arms. In 1930 it seems that H.M. Queen Elizabeth, the Queen Mother, has one of her own.* Bottom: *The bear as witness to adult tensions. Marcel Carné's 'Le Jour se lève', 1939.* Bottom corner: *Fetish, 1950.*

Adult relationships with teddy bears can range from mild interest to complete dependence. Even those who have not chosen to share their daily intimacies with a bear will nearly always betray signs of curiosity or genuine involvement. When teddy bears are displayed in an exhibition, visitors always want to touch and stroke them as inevitably they provoke an infinite number of childhood memories. No one can be so proud that they resist some exclamation of tenderness or some sentimental reminiscence; the emotional charge the teddy bear provokes amongst adults is undeniable. To rediscover one's teddy bear – or one like him – is to conjure up stories which are punctuated by signs of regret as the days of childhood resurface in flashes of startling clarity. The glimpse of a teddy bear in a shop window, a fleeting apparition, is a frustrating experience which is often enough to stimulate a sudden and irrepressible desire to search out and reclaim one's own beloved specimen.

Some adults involve their bear in a fantasy life, transforming him into a companion or partner who shares their private life and also, at times, their

When I was little and I went to mass on Sunday, they kept on saying: 'God is always with you.' That was why, each evening, I divided my bed into three parts. The outside was for my teddy, the middle was for God and the space next to the wall was for me.

All evening I stayed curled up, crushed against the wall. In the morning I was horrified to find that my teddy was on the floor and I was lying on top of God.

Adrian. Aged 14.

career. The owner virtually transforms the bear into a living being, attending to his every need (from the most basic to the most refined), dressing him, chatting to him, taking him to work and out on expeditions. Some people will reserve a hotel bedroom for their bear, others will tell their friends to speak softly because their bear has a headache, and others again will arrange their

Right: *Rather than being one owner's exclusive property, the bear is often passed on from one generation to another so that his loyalties are shared between a number of children.* Left: *the bear is often the first object in which the child finds total enjoyment.*

entourage of bears in the best seats at a first night without thinking twice about the audience's reaction. This bizarre and aberrant behaviour, a form of frustrated fetishism, is acted out in rituals. The adult here views the rituals in the samé way the child would; the bear's status is just as important as it would have been for the child. Such behaviour may be symptomatic of a need to prolong an interrupted childhood, or of an inability to accept adulthood, or even of a desire for a different, idealized alter ego. But, whatever the case, it demonstrates the tenacious affection even some *adults* feel for the stuffed bear.

Adults are not always so openly demonstrative, however, and sometimes seek refuge in their teddy bear only during times of crisis or mental anguish. In *L'Eté Meutrier* the young girl searching for her father openly displays her immaturity and emotional problems and carries a teddy bear under her arm. Fassbinder's film, *Despair*, which deals with the problems of identity and the notion of a double, ends as life ends and madness begins. The disorientated main character, awaiting arrest and imprisonment, is immersed in a paradoxical and unexpected

Stuffed bears interest me really because I have never personally owned one. Two complementary reasons led to this state of affairs. Firstly my parents sold teddies, and then also, from an early age, I cultivated a rational, scientific scepticism which, I must confess, was something of an affectation. I refused to believe that it was possible to become attached to a mass-produced companion but despite my example, my youngest brother happily accepted a bear as a present. It is easy enough to mock in the daylight, but when I found myself alone in bed knowing that my brother had company, I felt completely abandoned. It is better to swallow one's pride than to have to carry on swallowing tears. One only has to think of Galileo (who preferred to give up his theory rather than be separated for ever from other men) to see the way that great figures in history have put their *pride aside. That night, however, there was no bear with me to consummate my change of heart. Couldn't my bolster, which had soaked up my tears, respond to my affection just as well? . . . Through 'pillow talk' we came to an agreement, and I fell asleep clasping it in my arms. The bolster, unfortunately, had no arms. [. . .] In the morning I was somehow inspired by a new strength and decided I could do just as well without a bolster as a teddy, and without a bolster I have been, more or less, until today.*

Patrick Ravella.

Left: *A drawing by Berjac showing that the bear is a symbol of love which retains its hold even over adults.* Right: *The bear's enormous popularity has led to the making of a large number of more or less competent home-made models. This is a prototype velvet bear, dating from 1930.*

HISTOIRES NATURELLES
L'HOMME QUI A VU L'HOMME
QUI A VU L'OURS
Même
les chasseurs les
plus endurcis le
pressentent :
le jour où il n'y
aura plus d'ours
dans les Pyrénées,

conversation with a bear. In *Le Jour se Lève* it is a teddy bear who witnesses a young couple tearing each other apart and is the object of their tensions.

For some, the company of their own childhood teddy bear or the chance discovery of a stuffed bear is not enough; they experience an overwhelming desire to surround themselves with as many bears as possible, and also with the finest and rarest specimens. These are the collectors. Although all are prey to the same mania, they come in different types. Those who search out bears which are malformed, torn, patched-up or transformed into statuettes – in other words, precious talismans saved from oblivion – are very different from those who collect valuable bears which have become highly prized antiques. These astute investors are always on the look-out for labels hidden in the bear's ear and for the earliest manufacturer's trademarks, identifying a prize find.

As with all such pursuits, one of the attractions of hunting rare bears is the difficulty of finding the genuine article. Loved, lost, mislaid, occasionally abandoned in an act of exorcism, regarded as an investment to be carefully looked after in the hope of a decent profit, the teddy bear eventually finds himself transformed into a valuable object welcome even in the most famous of salerooms.

Until recently, arctophilia was limited to the English-speaking world but Europe and Japan in their turn have been smitten by teddy bears, although their appreciation falls somewhat short of the sort of veneration which certainly abounds elsewhere. Thousands of people attend conventions, picnics and rallies (as popular as rock concerts) accompanied by one or more of their many teddy bears. In these large crowds, where claws and snouts are held close to hands and faces, it is very hard to tell who is in control of whom and who has brought whom. The object of the exercise is to choose the oldest, the fattest, the smallest and the most valuable teddy bear – the list of honours for which the bears can compete is endless and competition is fierce. Such rallies are quite often organized by charities, because they have realized the potential media appeal of bears. Who better than a teddy bear to tug at people's emotions, when the teddy bear's primary function has always been that of a comforting presence? Here, then, the bear represents a combination of values – materialism and charity. In Japan, where dolls are believed to have a spiritual existence – being feared and respected intermediaries between man and the spiritual world – they are annually blessed in certain temples. Moreover, ceremonies are held there to assuage the souls of broken or worn-out dolls, and teddy bears are seen in the same light now. In America too, bear mania has created a world revolving around the teddy bear. There, stuffed bears have their own doctors, nurses and hospitals, their own newspapers, their own school uniforms and their own boutiques . . . The more rational European attitude resists the excessive, trivial and obsessive behaviour of this world which has become a virtual slave to its own mythologies.

Right: *A still from 'Company of Wolves', evidence to suggest that bears, like the wolf, form part of the mythology of fantastic woodland beasts . . . but the teddy bear is not so scary.*

THE BEAR AS A WORK OF ART

As a result of play, of wear and tear, and of daily use the teddy bear is transformed into an instant, ready-made work of art, worthy of a place in a museum. The affection and anger focused on a new bear alters him and the metamorphosis he undergoes is sometimes so great that he takes on the properties of some sort of ancient primitive sculpture. The basic definition of *art brut*, as set out by its high priest, Jean Dubuffet, springs to mind: 'All forms of production – drawings, paintings, needlework, modelled or sculpted figures etc. – offering a spontaneous and highly inventive appearance as little related as possible either to conventional art or to cultural clichés and produced by anonymous figures who are uninvolved in professional artistic circles.' It is because of children's unique, unpredictable and very personal method of 'working' that they can be seen to be practising a form of *art brut*; they have the same sense of joy and urgency in their work as their older colleagues in the art world. However, the gestures through which the bear has been reshaped over the years originates in impulses far removed from aesthetics; they are much more closely rooted in the satisfaction to be gained from imposing one's personality on a material object. However mutilated, malformed or dog-eared they may become, teddy bears retain their dignity, with their beady eyes and their snout held high. Their grave and rather pathetic demeanour, steeped in infinite nostalgia, means that few teddy bears have that world-weary outlook of embittered old men: many radiate a good humour born of the wisdom of years, often accumulated over several generations. Their worn-out coat, their missing limbs, their flattened head and mis-shapen features all bear eloquent testimony to their experience. Some are admittedly only a pale reflection of their former selves – so battered are they – but they still proudly proclaim that they are members of the teddy bear family. They speak to us of the passage and the irreversibility of time. Each bear is surrounded by a mysterious personal aura which conjures up a reminder of the child we have been or the adult we have become. Whether it is positive or negative charges that are given off, the sense of attraction or repulsion inspired by a teddy bear can scarcely leave us indifferent. Each one of us reacts differently as, in meeting them today, we are reminded of a former life. It explains the magnetic attraction they seem to exude and the familiarity with them that we fleetingly experience.

Left: *Metamorphosis.* Right: *Tired out from too much love.* Previous page: *A precious talisman.*

Worn out by too much Love

In *art brut*, great stress is laid upon the importance of bodily or gestural

manipulation within the creative process, ritual movements or repeated gestures sometimes being relied upon to produce the finishing touches. In the same way, in the child's relationship with his bear, it is through the continual repetition of certain gestures that a unique end-product is created out of the stiff, unyielding new bear. Some bears are worn smooth by all the love and affection lavished on them; by being ritually stroked and sucked the bear is modelled into a new shape. Like a stubborn, obsessive sculptor who knows that only time – like the patient ebb and flow of the tide – will impart a perfect polish to stone, so the child unwittingly goes about his task, day by day. His hand seems to move unconsciously, wearing away the fur to reveal the secrets of the warp and fibres. These bears, with their almost transparent skin and their straw or motley cotton wool entrails exposed, look like the primitive statuettes or tiny totems produced by unknown civilizations at an unspecified time in history. They give the impression of having been held in awe as talismans possessing supernatural powers. As a result, after several years, bears made by the same manufacturer never look entirely the same. Though they may share the same basic shape and features, their faces and psychological characteristics are different – rather like two non-identical twins. Having been held differently at night, their bodies sag in different places; different parts have been gnawed and sucked, neither their paws nor their ears have been subjected to the same rituals – each has led a separate life. With four limbs, a head and a pair of ears to be manipulated, there are, if not infinite, then considerable possible permutations of a teddy bear's shape, making each one a unique object.

Winnie-the-Pooh is one such bear. In 1920, when the Milne family gave Christopher Robin his little companion, all bears had standardized features, with distended snouts and long limbs. But Pooh does not look like this at all. His stomach is rounded, his muzzle is flat and, although his arms are long, his legs are short and stubby. The bear immortalized in Shepard's drawings is not a standard toy but one who has had its character shaped by its young owner.

In common with other creators of *art brut*, children have a great talent for drawing on a wide range of resources. Impelled by the need to create, the properties and appearance of different materials are less important than the urge to create itself. The evident need to impose their own identity on something often leads children to modify their stuffed toy by using unexpected materials and techniques, differentiating surfaces by giving each a characteristic texture. Occasionally one comes across bears who have been so greatly altered that they now look faintly amusing or even absurd. Some take on the guise of amulets; they are stuffed, or arrayed with a variety of objects suggestive of some mysterious symbolic power, which does not alter the bear's role as a toy, but instead gives it an added dimension.

The creator of *art brut* satisfies his creative urge by using in his work anything interesting he might happen to come across. The child is determined to adapt his bear by adding things which will make it his own; more often than not this means pieces of material, bandages, bits of string, ribbons or even an

A remodelled bear. Inexpert hands have tacked on patches from old overalls to save his skin, an operation completed with safety pins and pieces of elastoplast. The bear is stuffed with old straw and bits of wool, making him look something like a primitive statuette.*

Art Brut – The Ups and Downs Of A Teddy Bear

When I first saw them, I was perched in a display case on the top of a pile of useless objects at the back of an antique shop; I was only there because the owner of the shop valued me for the profit he expected from my sale.

There was no mistaking their expression of recognition. The sale was quickly made – there was a little haggling, a bit of sales patter and the money changed hands. I left my anonymity for an uncertain future.

I began to wonder about my new owners with some anxiety as they betrayed every sign of pleasure, and even a certain sense of triumph, at my acquisition. What was it they found so touching? Was it my worn-out coat, the repairs to my nose or my poor old legs, which had been patched up again and again where they had split open? I listened hard, opening the ears which, in the past, had heard so many secrets and sadnesses. On the face of it, it seemed as if they realised that I was not meant to be stuffed in the back of a cupboard or shown off in some junk shop. But I was intrigued when I heard them say: 'What a wonderful example of *art brut*.' For such were the strange new terms they used to talk about me. I was not entirely happy with the word 'example', but it was not really too bad. Anyway, now they had changed the subject and were talking about salerooms and prices. I was flattered by this mysterious word '*art*', but the sense of pride with which it filled me almost immediately disappeared, leaving me deflated, when it was followed by the word '*brut*'.

old rag that he might have sucked as an infant. Unable to part with this favourite item the child ensures that it becomes part of its successor – the bear. Affection can then be lavished on both cloth 'comforter' and bear at the same time. These cloth accessories, generally tied around the bear's neck, are vaguely reminiscent of those beautiful, brightly coloured bows worn by the bear when he was new, although instead of being decorative and faintly ridiculous, these new additions are playful and magical. They are a form of umbilical cord tying the child to his stuffed bear, they are new points of contact that secure the bear to its owner in an emotional ritual. When not made of some form of cloth, these additions range from pieces of broken toy to something stolen or borrowed from the adult world, secretly stuffed away and hidden in the teddy bear's abdomen, which often conceals many mysteries.

Top: *Bears whose limbs have fallen off after years of being played with.* Bottom: *Worn smooth by constant stroking.* Left: *The tears in his skin hastily repaired, the bear is rapidly restored to a uniquely beautiful object when back with the child, his ears being nibbled again.*

The teddy bear's unique, and somewhat disconcerting appearance is the result of the free-spirited imagination. The logic followed by both the creator of *art brut* and by the child adapting a teddy bear often escapes us. The end-product may either intrigue or disturb us, make us laugh or feel afraid, but it will never leave us indifferent.

At the Risk of Losing One's Skin

A child's fits of temper and rage have much in common with certain artists' wild and anti-social behaviour. Certainly, some teddy bears seem to have been in the wars: one-eyed, missing an arm or a leg, they carry the scars of having been at the receiving end of infantile aggression. This terrifying troop of truncated torsos, like the pieces of a puzzle, reveal their owners' more violent side, illustrating as eloquently as many artists' work the projection of impulses normally held in check or repressed. Some bears – broken, torn, dismembered – show the signs of being the object of more than mere tantrums or peevishness. Their role seems more akin to that of the dolls manufactured in China and Japan which are bought solely to be thrown into the river as a means of exorcising pain. Likewise teddy bears, used as emotional punchbags by children in moments of stress, act as a form of safety valve, becoming intermediaries between the child and the symbolic wound he has suffered; the child wishes to exorcise the pain, and the bear, as part of the child, suffers for his owner.

THE RED BARON

I was only just a year old when my father brought the Red Baron back to the house. If he was laid on his back, he made a strange noise, more like a cow's moo than anything resembling a bear's cry. [. . .]

The howl of protest I let out the first time that the Red Baron made his alpine moan was provoked less by any concern for authenticity than by fear. However much my parents tried to imitate this bovine bear's wailings, I remained unmoved. Quite the opposite, in fact. Watching them compete with the toy to make more and more sad and mournful noises upset me. Even the tiny vibration which seemed almost to send a slight shiver down the bear's back each time he cried out seemed rather unpleasant. After several failed attempts to leave the Baron in my cot with me when I went to sleep – I threw him out over the side or, if I failed to do that, I would turn bright red in a full-blooded tantrum – my mother decided to operate on the beast. Whether it was so that I should not miss the show, or whether it was to punish me for making her spoil a new toy, she sat me down at the table where the torture was to take place. With a jab of her scissors, she punctured the Red Baron's abdomen. Commenting all the while on his uncomplaining heroism – proof of the terrible pain he was suffering – and telling me how much more patient teddy bears were than children (both remarks having the desired effect of making me feel bad), she succeeded in removing from his stomach a small, square, metal box, perforated with tiny holes like a tea strainer. This was the source of the Baron's mournful song. The box was thrown into a dustbin, just like a discarded human organ after a hospital operation, and I never saw it again.

My mother comforted the Baron and ostentatiously sewed up his wound from top to bottom with black thread, which stood out against his honey-coloured fur and gave him the spurious appearance of a martyred bear. His red trousers, which had been spoilt by the operation, were thrown away too and from then on the Baron remained silent and naked, dressed only in his vertical scar.

Michel Braudeau
Naissance d'une passion.

This bear's insides are completely exposed. Bits of stuffing and metal spill out from the gap in his side. The handle is a pathetic reminder of a musical box which has now fallen silent. The autopsy has either been carried out by the ravages of time or, more probably, by prying and curious little hands.

The Little Household God

One of *art brut*'s characteristics is that it 'evades notions of private property and its ideological connotation – the work as an emanation of the individual'. Once a child has left home, if his bear is not jealously guarded in his bedroom, it is passed on from generation to generation, its features adapted and changed as each consecutive owner leaves his mark. The more a bear has been loved, the more children whose companion he has been, the more venerable and prized he is. He becomes like an elderly relative of the household rather than being an object of childhood memories. He is a constant link in a chain of love, his position and status similar to that of a pagan household god, protecting successive generations.

The Adult Sets Out to Reconquer Ruined Lands

There comes a day, however, when the bear becomes so dilapidated that it is necessary for an adult to work away at the plush and thus ensure that he still has a future. Once the stitching has given way and the stuffing begins to fall out, when a limb has come adrift or is in need of urgent attention, then the child calls upon adult skills. The task is not to be taken lightly. The parent has been given custody of a treasured toy and has been asked to ensure the survival of an irreplaceable object: it is a difficult task – one not dissimilar to playing with life and death. The child is all too aware of the potential loss, realizing that what he is asking for is the gift of eternal life for his bear, even though he only has a vague idea of what sort of great game is being played.

Faced with such a demand, the parent responds not only to the child's desire to recapture times past but also to his own instincts. He is struggling against the anguish of time, dissolution and the void. To lose the bear would be to lose Childhood with a capital 'C' – his own as well as the child's. It would serve to wipe out memories and rupture the chain of love handed down from generation to generation. The bear must be repaired. In many instances, the parent acts before the child has to ask, because she (or he) is worried and saddened by the toy's pathetic state, its uncertain future and its imminent decay. Anticipating a plea for help from the bear's owner and inspired by some sort of fellow feeling, the parent decides quite independently to postpone the demise of the much-loved toy.

The erosion of time confronts the adult's knowledgeable hand. A needle and thread come to the rescue; tackling the most threadbare patches, the hand's expertise manages to rebuild from next-to-nothing. It is through this restorative art, this knowledge oblivious to its own nature, but a knowledge which, nevertheless, works its own magic, that the adult too can claim to play a role in establishing the toy as a feature in the aesthetic ledger of *art brut*. There is something impressive about bears whose exteriors are really nothing but a tissue of scars, some stitched up clumsily, their seams bulging and distended, others showing the signs of expert attention, stitched together in matching thread almost invisible to the eye.

Bottom: *The joyful gesture leaves its mark – either by changing the bear's shape or by giving him a new appearance in paint.* Right: *With a wild gesture, the bear flies vertiginously forward. The line's energy matches the energy of the gesture; the child's gesture is as uncontrolled as the bear's.*

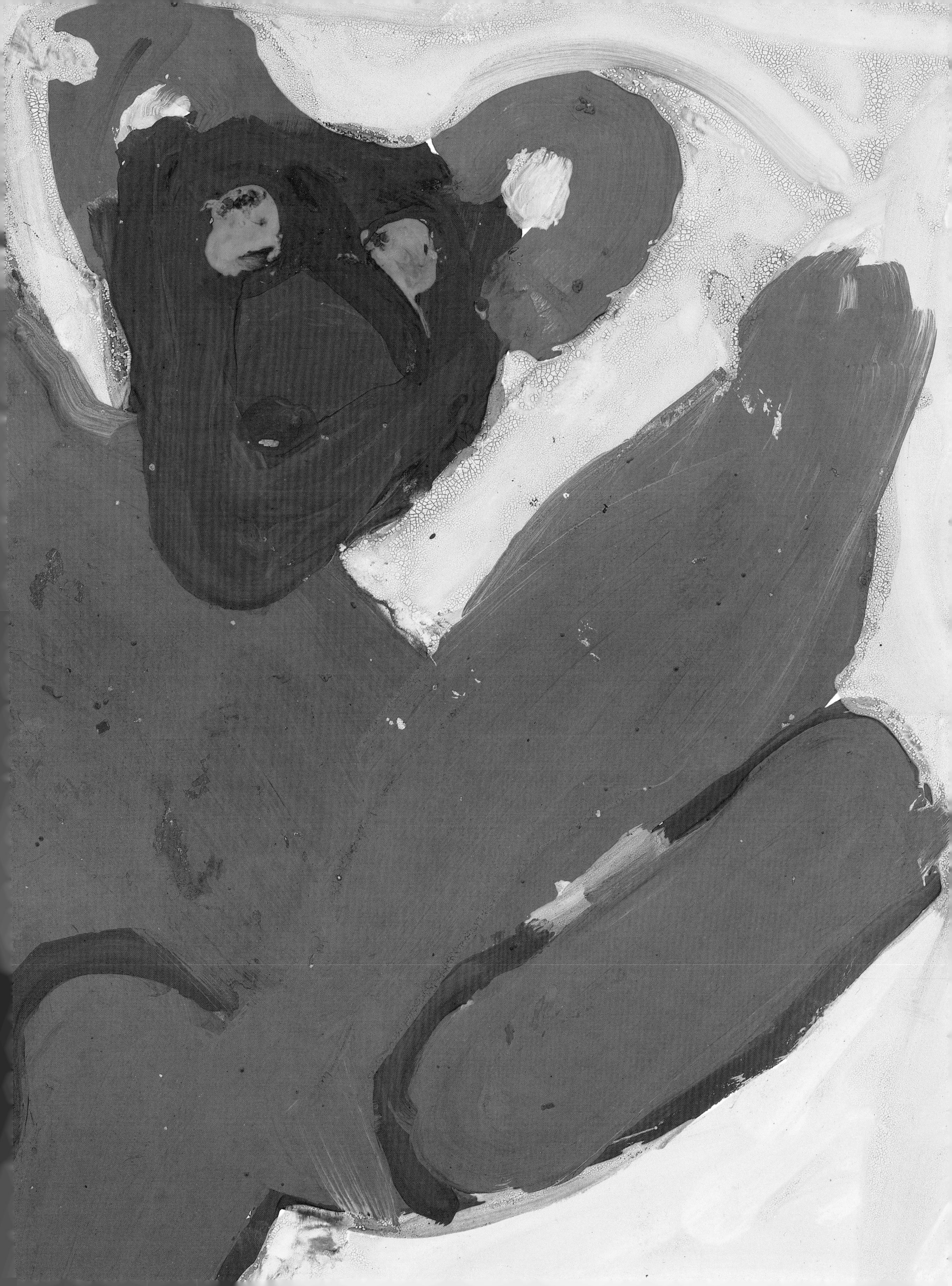

When there are more gaping wounds to deal with, loving hands will make a patch from another piece of material to stop the loss of stuffing which will otherwise signal the eventual demise of the bear. The dispersal of the actual body fabric must be overcome at any price, the skin which contains the essence of the bear's personality must be saved. As a result, some bears are small masterpieces of patchwork – a riot of baroque multi-colour patterns or more sober shadings. Shrewd repair work might leave only one leg moveable, but the other, happy enough merely to be attached to the torso once again, is scarcely concerned with mobility. Carefully drawn paper patterns may allow the reconstruction of an ear or an arm. It may be that the resulting replacement is either too long or too short, so that the bear suffers from an assymetry which clearly indicates that a transplant has taken place, but the most important thing is that just about everything has survived to ensure the child's continued friendship with his bear. However skilled or clumsy, the adult's surgery on the stuffed bear demonstrates a stubborn will to keep restoring the toy until the material, the threads, and finally even the filaments of each thread are completely beyond salvation.

Top: *The umbilical cords which tie the bear to its owner. The faces – flattened by innumerable hugs – bear testimony to a long-standing friendship.* Bottom: *This bear still has just enough characteristic features to prove that he is indeed a bear.*

Safety regulations imposed on stuffed toy manufacturers have had an effect on children's behaviour, so that the toy's natural evolution into a piece of primitive sculpture has been altered. Today it is practically impossible to pull out a bear's nose or eyes, or to pull off his ears. Changes in the material from which bears are made and in the shape of their features means that they do not age in the same way either. Because they are often made in one piece, they can no longer suffer amputation, and their long synthetic fur – washable and indestructible – arrogantly shrugs off signs of wear. Even when threadbare, the bears manufactured over the last twenty years are less attractive in old age. They somehow fail to attain the spiritual heights with which their ancestors were infused. Nowadays it is much harder for teddy bears as they grow old to catch the eye, speak to the soul and take on the disturbing, secret beauty of strange statuettes . . . Once, on the other hand it required no effort at all – it was a natural development.

Bear, Unique Piece, Mixed Materials, 1977

The teddy bear belongs to the world of objects by virtue of the methods by which he is produced, whether manufactured industrially or by hand. Industrial production-line techniques deny him the uniqueness conferred by hand-made manufacture, which places him within quite another artistic milieu – that of popular art. There is always an appealing awkwardness to hand-made bears; even when their proportions are impeccable and their appearance beyond reproach, there is something in their handmade quality – something a little extra – which is appealing. The knitted bears found at fairs and charity sales look more like cats or rabbits, and their loose stitching often leaves their stuffing exposed. Others have sausage-shaped limbs, their makers evidently having experienced some difficulty in producing properly rounded contours.

Left: *Childish fingers have played with and caressed this bear until his fur has been worn away. Exhausted by being cuddled at night, he is now transformed into a magical statuette able to withstand the passage of time.* Following page: *Patches and stitches demonstrate just how doggedly this threadbare teddy has been restored.*

Some are endowed with monstrous extremities, grotesque protruberances whose only virtue is that they allow the bear to stand up. Carelessly stuffed bears develop incongruous and strangely situated humps. Insofar as it is the expression of a social class, of its culture, its desires and its practical skills, the bear designed and made in the home can be considered a popular art object.

Non-commercial manufacture entails a form of creative process motivated by a desire to transform, manipulate and control matter according to personal ideals. The teddy bear provides an opportunity to transcend routine because he is an object which 'escapes' the hum-drum of daily life, and so takes part in the free play of energy.

The bear's ephemeral nature is also characteristic of popular art; he is essentially temporary and perishable, both in the material from which he is fashioned and the means by which he is assembled. Even when he is put together competently – be it naïve but shrewd or instinctively expert – the materials used to make him up are either already well worn or adapted for use in a way which appears disconcerting, both elements which would suggest that his lifespan is likely to be shorter than that of a commercially made bear.

Bears knitted out of wool oddments are a reincarnation of family pullovers; when sewn together, the old clothes are given new life. All too often one encounters bears made out of pieces of rabbit skin or fashioned from an old piece of faded and crumbling oil-cloth. Yet whatever materials are to be used, manufacturing techniques are modest in their demands on raw materials. Once the skin has been chosen, there are only three things to do: buttons must be chosen for the eyes, the other necessary facial appendages for smell and hearing must be embroidered and the stuffing must be added.

Generally such bears are made in one piece, and are usually made out of cloth. In their signs of wear they innocently carry memories – part of the very language of textiles. Even when the bear's skin is not made of cloth, his stomach is likely to be stuffed with old rags. Whether willingly or not, the bear thus takes his place in the family's vestimentary history, bearing witness to the rigours of daily life by displaying its battered stock of material oddments.

Although the first industrially produced bear appeared in 1903, there is no reason to believe that earlier versions do not exist. The dating of home-made bears is difficult, as the idiosyncracies of hand-crafted production cannot provide useful clues to machine manufacture, multiplication and trademarks.

Margarete Steiff's story is about the evolution of an industrial success which originated in the production of a hand-made object. At the time when the stuffed bear was invented, Steiff was already a well-known and flourishing company, but the teddy bear became so popular because Margarete Steiff herself had added to it her own personal touch. Margarete used to collect engravings and illustrations – perhaps it was in these that she found the inspiration for the elephant pincushion she made in 1880, which in turn led to the invention of the teddy bear. It was thus a characteristically popular craft-based mode of artistic production which lay behind what was to prove a great commercial success.

Mrs Michtom's work in America also follows a characteristically popular evolution, for there too the teddy bear craze grew out of humble, domestic beginnings. Before she was asked by her husband to produce a commercial prototype in order to test the market, she had produced stuffed toys, dolls and other animals. These were shrewdly exhibited as one-off models in the family's shop window to tempt customers who had come to buy sweets. It was Mrs Michtom too who made the bear which was to be sent to the White House, the one which seduced Theodore Roosevelt and decided the teddy bear's fate.

It is clear that some periods encourage the production of home-made bears more than others: they seem to breed in moments of crisis, poverty and war, when the adult forgets his own difficulties in order to satisfy his children's needs. The home-made bear is beginning to disappear now as a result of such factors as lack of time, and the fact that mass-produced, cheap toys are now widely available in department stores. Yet social and cultural factors are still responsible for those which *are* made. Over the last twenty years, interest in different aspects of 'do-it-yourself' has become so widespread that one can almost speak of a 'handmade' generation. A range of specialist magazines caters for, and exploits the craft-orientated tastes cultivated by the children of the Sixties and Seventies. As a result, patterns for stuffed bears are still occasionally produced to enable enthusiasts to make their own teddy bears.

Looking even more closely, it is obvious that the making of home-made bears changes and adapts according to circumstances. While the aim, in times of need, is to produce a bear which looks like a manufactured toy, in times of plenty it is originality and differentiation which becomes all important. Even though our generation is one of industrious self-helpers, who may have given up making their own furniture and their own jam, the social changes which have resulted have not affected the production of teddy bears. They are still made for two real reasons, to satisfy a desire to create something and, above all, to make children happy.

Some time later, when I was two years old, I discovered that the Red Baron had two sides to his character. When it was light – either in the sunshine or in the glow of my bedside lamp – he looked like a good-natured, disembowelled bear. But he seemed quite different in the dark. The slightest ray of light prevented me from seeing his other face and I tried in vain to look at him when it was dark, because I could never stay awake long enough to discover what he looked like when he knew I was not looking. Perhaps it was then that he spoke, or maybe whispered. Or perhaps he just transmitted his thoughts to me when I lay defenceless and asleep. I thought I could hear a harsh, nasal voice, one that became familiar in later years when I heard the rapid, clipped tones of Louis Jouvet at the cinema. It was a voice which came from inside, and which only I could hear; but nobody ever seemed to be surprised by what the Red Baron said to me. At first, he complained about the part he played within the household and about his colour: he thought he was green rather than red, but he was happy to accept his name and the affection I showed towards him. He passed comment on the day which had just ended, made rather unflattering comments about our neighbours in Providence and relished indiscreet gossip.

When I was asleep he really got going, speaking in a sharp, secretive tone that I could never resist. He was responsible for putting most of the wicked thoughts into my head, which had been inspired by the religious imagery we had in the house. He was always on Satan's side; he was always telling me how friendly and easy-going Satan was. He would praise his fantastic imagination and good sense. 'Of course, my dear Axel,' he would say, 'you have nothing to gain from this religious self-denial – it's a waste of time. Don't throw away your life in pointless work, when you can steal or find someone else willing to exhaust themselves on your behalf. And, most important of all, don't hesitate to be disobedient. Personally, I would give you every encouragement.'

Michel Braudeau
Naissance d'une passion.

Design: Marc Walter

The authors would like to thank: The Toy Museum, Poissy - The Firms: Anima, Boulgam, Alfa, Thiennot, Steiff - Cecile, Pascale and Pierre Frenay - Catherine Fel - Fabienne Vaslet - Marc Walter - Corinne Pauvert - Adrien Bertrand - Lasailly - Gilbert Coudene - Patrick Ravella - François-Xavier Bouchart - Max Barboni - André Bouilly - Martine Rossiaud - Nathalie des Gayets - Georgette and Guy Gauchon - Gisèle and Bernard Picot- Monsieur Eimermann - Denis Hyenne - The Guerret Family and all those of our friends who are collectors of bears...
We also thank Bella Cohen, Michel Braudeau and Jean Fléchet.

Acknowledgements

Naissance d'une passion by Michel Braudeau, © Editions du Seuil, *110, 119*; *Le Montreur d'ours* by Jean Fléchet, Atelier du Gué, *44*; *Belle du Seigneur*, by Albert Cohen, © Editions Gallimard, *89*.

Photographic Acknowledgements

Boulgom Archives, *38 top*; Steiff Archives, *16*; Archives of the Musée du Jouet, Passy, *86*; © Max Barboni 1987, *28, 29 right, 54, 64, 75, 84, 102–3, 111, 114, 118*; © Francois-Xavier Bouchart 1987, *5, 11, 17, 19 bottom, 20–1, 26–7, 29 left, 30, 34–5, 50, 58–60, 63, 67–8, 71, 88 centre, 99, 104–5, 107–8, 116*; Berjac, *98*; The Bettmann Archive Inc., *10, 19 top, 25*; © Central Press Photos Ltd, *94*; © Jean-Claude Couval 1987, *91*; 'Cahiers du Cinéma' documentation, *101*; Cinéstar documentation, *94 bottom*; M. Eimermann, *80–1*; Ellan, *1*; © Fox Photos 1987, *18*; © Gamma 1987, *92*; Sander, *100*; Gauchon collection, *83*; Geneviève Gauchon-Picot, *109*; Louis-Amélie Guerret, *2–3, 78–9*; Denis Hyère collection, *76–7*; © Magnum, *93 top*; de Andrade, *93 bottom*; Davidson – Publicité Agence Etrangère, *24*; © Roger-Viollet 1987, *49*; © Koren Trygg – Exclamations Incorporated, *8–9*.

Illustration Acknowledgements

Monsieur Ours fétiche by Maby, *15 top*; drawing by Samivel from *Bruno l'ours*, © Librairie Delagrave 1939, *42*; illustration by V. Floyd Campbell for *The Roosevelt Bear*, Seymour Eaton, 1906, *43*; illustration by J.-M. Nicollet for Mark Twain's *How I Killed a Bear*, © Editions Gallimard, collection Enfantimages, *45*; illustration from Alain Saint-Ogan's *Mariage de Prosper*, © Librairie Hachette and Dimanche illustré 1936, *49 inset*; illustration by F.-G. Lewin from *Martin Jacquot et Cie*, © Hachette 1927, *55*; illustration by F. Rojankowsky for Marie Colmont's *Michka*, © Flammarion, Albums du Père Castor, *56*; © Express Newspapers p.l.c., *57*; 'Gros Nounours', created by Claude Laydu for the television programme 'Bonne nuit les petits', *57 top right*; Winnie-the-Pooh © the Walt Disney Company 1987, reproduced with special permission from Walt Disney Productions (France), *57 bottom*; drawings by E. H. Shepard, © according to the Berne Convention, *61*.

688.724 414987
Picot, Genevieve and Gerard
Bears

ST. MARYS PUBLIC LIBRARY
100 Herb Bauer Drive
St. Marys, GA 31558
882-4800
JAN 20 1993